PRESSURE COOKING

Edited by
Eileen Turner

CONTENTS

This edition first published 1978 by
Octopus Books Limited
59 Grosvenor Street, London W.1.

© 1978 Octopus Books Limited

ISBN 0 7064 0700 8

Produced and printed in Hong Kong by
Mandarin Publishers Limited
22a Westlands Road, Quarry Bay

Frontispiece: GOLDEN HARVEST CASSEROLE *(page 31),*
MIDSUMMER LAMB *(page 48) (Photograph: Taunton Cider)*

Weights and Measures

All measurements in this book are based on Imperial weights and measures, with American equivalents given in parenthesis.

Measurements in *weight* in the Imperial and American system are the same. Measurements in *volume* are different, and the following table shows the equivalents:

Spoon measurements

Imperial	U.S.
1 tablespoon	1 tablespoon
1½ tablespoons	2 tablespoons
2 tablespoons	3 tablespoons
	(abbrev: T)

Level spoon measurements are used in all the recipes.

Liquid measurements

1 Imperial pint	20 fluid ounces
1 American pint	16 fluid ounces
1 American cup	8 fluid ounces

INTRODUCTION

Although a pressure cooker is not a new piece of kitchen equipment, its advantages are becoming more widely appreciated as fuel costs rise and people find they have less time to spend in the kitchen. For many foods, cooking time is cut by 75% and once pressure is reached, only very low heat is needed to maintain it.

The majority of recipes in this book, therefore, are ones which take full advantage of the saving in time and fuel, so dishes which normally take a long time, such as soups, stews and steamed puddings tend to predominate. On the other hand, foods such as fish and chicken joints, which can provide a quickly prepared meal when cooked in a pressure cooker, are also included. There are also some quickly prepared desserts to complete the meal.

As different brands of pressure cooker vary in design, it is important to follow the manufacturer's instructions concerning the operation of the cooker. Pressure cookers which have only HIGH (15 lb.) pressure can be used for most of the recipes in this book. Although LOW (5 lb.) pressure is recommended for steamed puddings, HIGH (15 lb.) pressure can give good results as long as the pre-steaming instructions are followed.

When using the recipes in this book, always remove the trivet from the cooker unless the instructions state otherwise. Any watertight, heatproof containers may be used in a pressure cooker, but thin ones are preferable. If thick dishes are used, add a few minutes to the cooking time.

CHICKEN SOUP, *page 11 (Photograph: British Poultry Information Service)*

SOUPS AND STOCKS

General Purpose Stock

2 lb. meat bones, fresh or from
  cooked meat
2 ½ pints (6 ¼ cups) water
2 celery stalks, chopped
2 onions, quartered

2 carrots, sliced
bouquet garni
1 teaspoon salt
6 peppercorns

Wash the bones and break them up as small as possible. Put them in the pressure cooker with the water, making sure that the cooker is not more than half full. Bring to the boil in the open cooker and remove the scum with a slotted spoon. Add the rest of the ingredients, put on the lid and bring to HIGH (15 lb.) pressure. Cook for 30 minutes if the bones are from cooked meat, 45 minutes if they are fresh.

   Reduce pressure at room temperature. Strain the stock, leave it to cool and skim off fat before using.

   These quantities give a rich, concentrated stock which may be diluted with an equal quantity of water before use.

Brown stock:
Make as above but slice the onions and fry them in a little hot fat until brown, then drain them and add them to the cooker with the other ingredients.

Chicken Stock

cooked chicken carcass
1 onion, stuck with a clove
1 carrot, sliced
4 celery stalks, chopped
bouquet garni

thin strip of lemon rind
½ teaspoon salt
pinch of pepper
1 ½ pints (3 ¾ cups) water

Remove any meat from the carcass and cut it into small pieces. Break up the bones as small as possible. Put the bones, scraps of meat and skin in the cooker with the other ingredients and the water. Bring to the boil in the open cooker and skim off any froth. Put on the lid, bring up to HIGH (15 lb.) pressure and cook for 20 minutes.

   Reduce pressure at room temperature and strain the stock. Leave the stock to cool; when it is cold, skim off the fat. Dilute with an equal quantity of water before use.

Chicken Soup

cooked chicken carcass
1¼ pints (3 cups) water
bouquet garni
salt and pepper
½ lb. (1½ cups) carrots, sliced

4 oz. (¾ cup) frozen peas
¼ pint (⅔ cup) milk
¼ pint (⅔ cup) cream
chopped fresh parsley to garnish

Remove any meat from the carcass and cut it into small pieces. Put the carcass in the pressure cooker with the water, bouquet garni and seasoning. Bring to the boil and remove any scum with a slotted spoon. Put on the lid and bring to HIGH (15 lb.) pressure. Cook for 10 minutes.

Reduce pressure at room temperature. Strain the stock and return it to the cooker with the carrots. Bring to the boil and add the peas. Put on the lid and bring to HIGH (15 lb.) pressure. Cook for 4 minutes. Reduce pressure at room temperature. Return the cooker to the heat and add the milk and cream. Adjust seasoning and reheat until the soup just comes to the boil. Sprinkle with chopped parsley. Serve with French bread.
Serves 4

Cream of Celery Soup

1-1½ lb. celery, cleaned
2 small onions, sliced
1 oz. (2T) butter
¾ pint (2 cups) chicken stock
salt
2-3 peppercorns

For thickening:
1 oz. (2T) butter
1 oz. (¼ cup) flour
¼ pint (⅔ cup) milk
For serving:
finely chopped celery leaves
1 tablespoon (1T) cream per
   portion (optional)

Cut the washed celery into 1 inch lengths and set aside the smallest green leaves from the heart. Gently cook the onions in the butter in the open pressure cooker but do not allow them to brown. Add the stock, seasoning and celery. Bring to the boil, skim well and put on the lid. Bring to HIGH (15 lb.) pressure and cook for 10 minutes. Reduce pressure at room temperature and sieve the soup or purée in an electric blender.

Meanwhile, melt the butter in a large pan, add the flour and cook gently for 1 minute, stirring. Take the pan off the heat and add the milk, beating until the sauce is smooth. Stir in the soup. Return the pan to the heat, re-boil and cook gently for 5 minutes, stirring all the time. Serve sprinkled with the chopped celery leaves and pour the cream into each portion.
Serves 4

Curried Lamb Soup

¾ lb. scrag end of neck of lamb
2 tablespoons (3T) oil
1 onion, chopped
1 tablespoon curry powder
1¼ pints (3 cups) stock

8 oz. can (1 cup) tomatoes
1 apple
1 oz. (3T) raisins
2 tablespoons (3T) chutney

Cut the lamb into small pieces, discarding the bone and removing excess fat. Heat the oil in the pressure cooker and add the lamb and onion. Fry gently, uncovered, for about 4 minutes. Stir in the curry powder and cook for a further minute. Add the stock and tomatoes with their juice. Put on the lid and bring to HIGH (15 lb.) pressure. Cook for 7 minutes.

Reduce pressure at room temperature. Peel, core and chop the apple and add it to the cooker with the raisins and chutney. Adjust seasoning if necessary. Return the cooker to the heat, put on the lid and bring to HIGH (15 lb.) pressure. Cook for a further 3 minutes. Reduce pressure at room temperature.

This nourishing soup makes a meal in itself. Serve accompanied by side dishes of rice, crisp fried noodles and a tomato salad.
Serves 4

Rich Vegetable Soup

2 streaky bacon rashers (fatty
   bacon slices)
2 small onions, sliced
2 carrots, sliced
small piece of turnip, chopped
1 tablespoon flour

2 pints (5 cups) hot stock
2 celery stalks, chopped
2 tomatoes, skinned and finely
   chopped
bouquet garni
salt and pepper

Remove the rind from the bacon and cut the bacon into very small pieces. Cook it gently in the open pressure cooker until all the fat has run out. Then add the onions, carrots and turnip and fry until golden brown. Add the flour and cook for a minute or two, stirring all the time. Take the cooker off the heat, pour in the stock and add the remaining ingredients. Put on the lid and bring to HIGH (15 lb.) pressure. Cook for 5 minutes. Reduce pressure at room temperature.

Remove the bouquet garni, skim off the fat and adjust the seasoning. If a thick soup is wanted, strain it, sieve or purée the vegetables in an electric blender. Return the purée to the open cooker with the liquid and re-boil.
Serves 4-6

CURRIED LAMB SOUP *(Photograph: Bisto)*

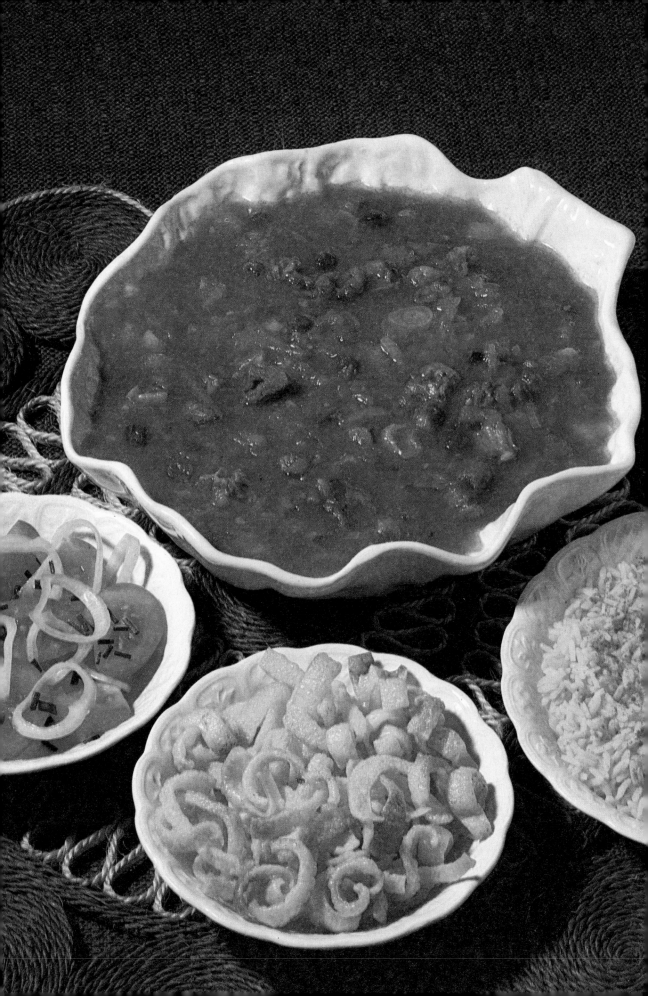

Carrot Soup

1 lb. carrots, sliced
1 celery stalk, chopped
1 small onion, sliced
½ lb. potatoes, diced
1 garlic clove, crushed
1 oz. (2T) butter
1 ¼ pints (3 cups) water

1 bay leaf
salt and pepper
½ pint (1 ¼ cups) milk
2 tablespoons (3T) double
  (heavy) cream
chopped fresh parsley to garnish

Lightly fry the vegetables and garlic in the melted butter in the open pressure cooker until they are soft. Add the water, bay leaf and seasoning. Put on the lid and bring to HIGH (15 lb.) pressure. Cook for 10 minutes.

Reduce pressure at room temperature. Remove the bay leaf and sieve the soup or purée it in an electric blender. Return the soup to the cooker and add the milk. Reheat, uncovered, and bring it just to the boil, then take the cooker off the heat. Stir in the cream and parsley just before serving.
Serves 4

Spinach and Lentil Soup

6 oz. (¾ cup) lentils
½ lb. bacon (boiling ham),
  chopped
1 onion, sliced
1 teaspoon mixed dried herbs

pepper
2 pints (5 cups) water
11 oz. frozen spinach or 1 lb. fresh
  spinach

Put the lentils, bacon, onion, herbs and pepper in the pressure cooker with the water. Put on the lid and bring to HIGH (15 lb.) pressure and cook for 15 minutes.

Reduce pressure at room temperature. Wash the fresh spinach or break up the frozen spinach. Add the spinach to the cooker, put on the lid and bring to HIGH (15 lb.) pressure. Cook for a further 2 minutes. Reduce pressure at room temperature. Sieve the soup or purée it in an electric blender. If it is too thick, add a little milk and reheat. Adjust seasoning if necessary.
Serves 6
Note: If the bacon is salty, soak it for about 6 hours in cold water before using.

Fish Stock

cod's head, trimmings and bones
  left after filleting fish
1 carrot, sliced
1 onion, sliced

bouquet garni
thin strip of lemon rind
6 peppercorns
pinch of salt

Wash the fish head and put it in the pressure cooker with the other ingredients and enough water to cover — at least 1 pint (2½ cups). Bring to the boil in the open cooker and remove all the scum with a slotted spoon. Put on the lid and bring to HIGH (15 lb.) pressure. Cook for 15 minutes. Reduce pressure at room temperature and strain.

Use the stock on the day it is made.

Fish and Corn Chowder

½ lb. cod, skinned and cut into
  large pieces
2 onions, chopped
11½ oz. can (3 cups) sweetcorn
  (whole kernel corn)
1 pint (2½ cups) fish stock or water
1 tablespoon tomato purée
grated rind of 1 lemon

1 bay leaf
salt and pepper
¼ pint (⅔ cup) double (heavy)
  cream
Garnish:
lemon slices
few peeled prawns (shrimp)
chopped fresh parsley

Put the cod, onions, corn, stock or water in the cooker with the tomato purée, lemon rind, bay leaf and seasoning. Put on the lid and bring to HIGH (15 lb.) pressure. Cook for 5 minutes. Reduce pressure slowly. Discard the bay leaf. Stir in the cream and reheat gently. Garnish with lemon slices, prawns and parsley.
Serves 4-6

Minestrone

2 oz. (¼ cup) haricot (navy) beans
1 onion, chopped
3 celery stalks, chopped
½ small cabbage, shredded
1 leek, shredded
1 large potato, diced
1 garlic clove, crushed

14 oz. can (1¾ cups) tomatoes
2 pints (5 cups) stock or water
salt and pepper
2 oz. (⅓ cup) long grain rice
Garnish:
chopped fresh parsley
grated Parmesan cheese

Pour boiling water over the beans and leave them to soak for about 1 hour. Then drain the beans and put them in the cooker with the vegetables, garlic, tomatoes with their juice and the stock or water. Add salt and pepper. Put on the lid and bring to HIGH (15 lb.) pressure. Cook for 15 minutes.

Reduce pressure at room temperature. Return cooker to the heat, bring to the boil and add the rice. Put on the lid and bring to HIGH (15 lb.) pressure. Cook for a further 5 minutes. Reduce pressure at room temperature. Adjust seasoning if necessary. Add the chopped parsley and serve with grated Parmesan cheese.
Serves 6

Beef, Ham and Pasta Soup

1 lb. stewing beef, cut into small
  cubes
1 onion, chopped
1 oz. (2T) butter

1 ham bone
1 bay leaf
2 pints (5 cups) water
4 oz. (1 cup) pasta shells

Lightly fry the beef and onion in the melted butter in the open pressure cooker for 5 minutes. Add the ham bone, bay leaf and water. Put on the lid, bring to HIGH (15 lb.) pressure and cook for 7 minutes.

Reduce pressure at room temperature. Remove the bone and the bay leaf. Return cooker to the heat, bring soup to the boil and add the pasta. Bring to HIGH (15 lb.) pressure and cook for a further 3 minutes. Reduce pressure at room temperature. Serve with crusty bread.
Serves 4-6

MINESTRONE *(Photograph: Bisto)*

Oxtail Soup

1 oxtail, jointed
1 oz. (2T) butter
2 onions, chopped
2 celery stalks, sliced
1 carrot, sliced
1 oz. lean bacon, chopped

2 pints (5 cups) beef stock
bouquet garni
salt and pepper
1 oz. (¼ cup) flour
1 teaspoon lemon juice

Fry the oxtail pieces in the melted butter in the open pressure cooker for a few minutes, then add the vegetables and bacon and continue cooking until the oxtail is browned. Add the stock and bouquet garni, and season well. Put on the lid and bring to HIGH (15 lb.) pressure. Cook for 40 minutes. Reduce pressure at room temperature. Strain the soup, remove the meat from the bones and cut it into small pieces.

Leave the stock to cool, then skim off the surface fat. Return the stock to the cooker with the meat and reheat. Mix the flour with a little cold water to make a smooth paste. Add a little of the hot stock, then stir the mixture into the soup. Bring to the boil, stirring constantly. Add the lemon juice and adjust seasoning if necessary.

Serves 6-8

Bacon and Bean Soup

gammon (ham) knuckle, soaked
  overnight in water
4 oz. (½ cup) haricot (navy) beans
2 celery stalks, chopped
2 carrots, chopped
1 onion, chopped

1½ pints (3¾ cups) water
bouquet garni
½ pint (1¼ cups) milk, or milk and
  single (light) cream
chopped fresh parsley to garnish

Pour boiling water over the beans and leave them to soak for about 1 hour. Meanwhile strip the rind from the meat, remove meat from the bone and cut it into small pieces. Put the drained beans, the bone, meat and vegetables in the pressure cooker. Pour on the water and add the bouquet garni. Bring to the boil, uncovered, and remove any scum with a slotted spoon. Put on the lid, bring to HIGH (15 lb.) pressure and cook for 20 minutes.

Reduce pressure slowly. Take out the bouquet garni and the bone. Add the milk, or milk and cream, and reheat gently. Add the parsley before serving.

Serves 6-8

FISH

Cod in White Wine

1 ¼ lb. salt cod fillet
2 oz. (¼ cup) butter
2 lb. small new potatoes, scraped

2 onions, chopped
½ pint (1 ¼ cups) dry white wine
pinch of pepper

Soak the cod in cold water for 24 hours, changing the water frequently. Drain the fish and dry it with absorbent kitchen paper. Cut the cod into portions.

Melt the butter in the open pressure cooker and gently cook the potatoes and onions until they are slightly softened. Take out the vegetables and put them in a perforated separator. Cook the fish gently in the remaining butter, then return the vegetables to the cooker. Add the wine and the pepper and put on the lid. Bring to HIGH (15 lb.) pressure and cook for 5 minutes.

Reduce pressure in cold water. Lift out the cod carefully with a fish slice and place it on a warm serving dish. Arrange the vegetables round it and spoon the sauce over the top.
Serves 4

Fish Casserole

1½ lb. cod fillet
juice of 1 lemon
salt and pepper
4 oz. (1 cup) button mushrooms,
 sliced or chopped
1 medium-sized onion, chopped
1 small red pepper, chopped

½ lb. tomatoes, chopped
¼ pint (⅔ cup) fish stock
1 tablespoon brown sugar
1 oz. (2T) butter
2 tablespoons (3T) peas, cooked
2 tablespoons (3T) chopped fresh
 parsley

Divide the fish into portions and place it in the pressure cooker. Sprinkle lemon juice over the fish and season well. Scatter the mushrooms, onion and pepper over the fish and add half the tomatoes, skinned. Pour in the fish stock. Sprinkle the brown sugar over the top and add knobs of butter. Cover with a piece of greased greaseproof (waxed) paper.

Put the trivet in the pressure cooker with ½ pint (1¼ cups) water. Place the dish on the trivet, put on the lid of the cooker and bring to HIGH (15 lb.) pressure. Cook for 5 minutes. Garnish with the peas, the rest of the tomatoes and chopped parsley. Serve with crusty French bread.
Serves 4

Lemon Mackerel

4 mackerel, cleaned and boned
1 small onion, finely chopped
1 hard-boiled egg, chopped
1 tablespoon chopped fresh
 parsley

2 oz. (1 cup) fresh breadcrumbs
juice of 1 lemon
salt and pepper
milk to mix

Trim the heads, tails and fins from the fish. Mix the remaining ingredients to make a firm stuffing and fill the fish with it.

Pour ½ pint (1¼ cups) water into the pressure cooker. Butter the top of the trivet and place it in the cooker. Arrange the fish on the trivet. Put on the lid and bring to HIGH (15 lb.) pressure. Cook for 6 minutes. Reduce pressure in cold water.
Serves 4

FISH CASSEROLE *(Photograph: White Fish Authority)*

Soused Herrings or Mackerel

4 herrings or mackerel, cleaned
¼ pint (⅔ cup) vinegar
¼ pint (⅔ cup) water
1 onion, sliced
6 peppercorns
4 cloves
1 bay leaf

strip of lemon peel
1 garlic clove, peeled
pinch of salt
Garnish:
chopped capers or thinly sliced
   raw onion rings
chopped chives or parsley

Wash, trim and scale the fish and cut off the heads. Place the fish in the pressure cooker, top to tail. Pour over the vinegar and water. Add the onion, peppercorns, cloves, bay leaf, lemon peel, garlic and salt. Place a double thickness of greaseproof paper on top of the fish. Put on the lid and bring to HIGH (15 lb.) pressure. Cook for 6-8 minutes, according to size of the fish.

If serving the fish hot, reduce pressure in cold water. Lift the fish on to a serving dish and keep it hot. Boil the liquid in the cooker rapidly, uncovered, until it is reduced by half, then strain it over the fish. Garnish with capers and parsley or chives.

To serve the fish cold, reduce the cooker pressure at room temperature. Leave the fish in the cooker until it is quite cold, then lift it out and drain it. This can be done by placing it on the inverted trivet on a large plate. Boil the cooking liquor rapidly in the cooker, uncovered, until it is reduced by half and allow it to cool. The fish may be left whole or boned and divided into fillets. Place the fish on a serving dish and strain the cooled liquid over it. Serve with onion rings and chopped parsley.
Serves 4

Fish with Creole Sauce

1 ½ lb. plaice (flounder) fillets
2 tablespoons (3T) oil
1 small onion, chopped
1 garlic clove, crushed
1 celery stalk, chopped
1 green pepper, seeded and
  chopped
15 oz. can (scant 2 cups) tomatoes

1 tablespoon tomato purée
pinch of sugar
salt and pepper
pinch of dried basil
pinch of chilli powder
Garnish:
½ lemon, sliced
watercress

Skin the fillets and roll them up, starting from the tail end, and secure with string or wooden cocktail sticks. Heat the oil in the open pressure cooker and lightly fry the onion, garlic, celery and green pepper. Drain the tomatoes, retaining the juice. Make up the tomato juice to ½ pint (1¼ cups) with water and add it to the cooker with the tomatoes, tomato purée, sugar, seasoning, herbs and chilli powder. Place the rolled fish fillets in the cooker, put on the lid and bring to HIGH (15 lb.) pressure. Cook for 4 minutes.

Reduce pressure in cold water. Garnish the fish with lemon slices and watercress.
Serves 4

Stuffed Plaice or Sole

2 plaice (flounder) or sole, filleted
  and skinned
juice of ½ lemon
3 oz. (1 ½ cups) fresh white
  breadcrumbs

1 tablespoon chopped fresh
  parsley
1 hard-boiled egg, chopped
salt and pepper
2 oz. (¼ cup) butter, melted

Sprinkle the fish fillets with lemon juice. Mix together the breadcrumbs, parsley and egg. Season and bind the stuffing with the melted butter. Spread the stuffing over the skinned side of each fillet and roll up, starting from the tail end. Secure with string or wooden cocktail sticks (toothpicks).

Pour ½ pint (1¼ cups) water in the pressure cooker. Butter the top of the trivet and place it in the cooker. Arrange the fish on the trivet. Put on the lid and bring to HIGH (15 lb.) pressure. Cook for 8 minutes. Reduce pressure in cold water.
Serves 4

Macaroni Fish Pie

1 lb. haddock fillet, cut into 3
  pieces
juice of ½ lemon
salt and pepper
1 oz. (2T) butter
8 oz. (2 cups) short length
  macaroni
1 oz. (¼ cup) Cheddar cheese,
  grated

Cheese sauce:
1 oz. (2T) butter
1 oz. (¼ cup) flour
½ pint (1¼ cups) milk
salt and pepper
pinch of dry mustard
2 oz. (½ cup) Cheddar cheese,
  grated
sprig of parsley to garnish

Place the fish on buttered foil and sprinkle over the lemon juice and seasoning, then dot with butter. Make the fish into a parcel with the foil, sealing the edges carefully.

Put 2 pints (5 cups) water in the pressure cooker, add a little salt and put the fish parcel in. Bring the water to the boil and add the macaroni. Put on the lid and slowly bring to HIGH (15 lb.) pressure. Cook for 4 minutes.

While the fish and macaroni are cooking, make the sauce. Melt the butter in a pan, stir in the flour and cook for a minute or two. Remove the pan from the heat and stir in the milk and seasoning. Return the pan to the heat and bring to the boil, stirring all the time. When the sauce has thickened, lower the heat and add the cheese, stirring until it melts.

Reduce the cooker pressure in cold water. Flake the fish and add to the sauce. Strain the macaroni and add it to the fish and sauce. Place the mixture in a buttered flame-proof dish and sprinkle with grated cheese and melted butter. Brown under a hot grill (broiler) and garnish with parsley. Serve with broccoli.
Serves 4

MACARONI FISH PIE *(Photograph: White Fish Authority)*

POULTRY AND GAME

Chicken Casserole with Cider

4 chicken joints, thawed if frozen
2 oz. (¼ cup) butter
1 onion, chopped
1 oz. (¼ cup) flour
½ lb. button (cocktail) onions,
  peeled

½ lb. small whole carrots
½ pint (1¼ cups) dry cider
¼ pint (⅔ cup) chicken stock
salt and pepper
½ lb. (1½ cups) peas, cooked

Fry the chicken joints in the melted butter in the open pressure cooker until golden all over. Take the joints out and fry the chopped onion until soft. Then take the onion out and gently cook the flour in the remaining fat, stirring, until it is lightly coloured. Remove the flour and put it aside. Return the chicken and cooked onion to the cooker and add the whole onions and carrots. Pour in the cider and stock, and season well. Put on the lid and bring to HIGH (15 lb.) pressure. Cook for 6-8 minutes, according to size of the joints.

Reduce pressure in cold water. Return the cooker to the heat and stir in the cooked flour. Bring to the boil, stirring until the liquid thickens. Add the cooked peas and heat through. Serve in a warm casserole.
Serves 4

Chicken and Mushroom Casserole

2 oz. (¼ cup) butter
2 large onions, sliced
6 chicken drumsticks, thawed if frozen
1 tablespoon flour

½ lb. potatoes, diced
2 oz. (½ cup) mushrooms, sliced
½ pint (1¼ cups) chicken stock
bouquet garni
salt and pepper

Melt the butter in the open pressure cooker and gently fry the onion for 2-3 minutes. Toss the drumsticks in the flour and cook them with the onion until golden brown all over. Take the cooker off the heat and add the vegetables and the stock with the bouquet garni and seasoning. Put on the lid and bring to HIGH (15 lb.) pressure. Cook for 5 minutes. Reduce pressure in cold water. Remove the bouquet garni and serve.
Serves 4-6

Chicken Marengo

4 chicken joints, thawed if frozen
salt and pepper
2 tablespoons (3T) oil
1 onion, sliced
1 garlic clove, crushed
12 button mushrooms
4 tomatoes, skinned and quartered

½ pint (1¼ cups) white wine
¼ pint (⅔ cup) chicken stock
pinch of dried thyme
1 bay leaf
1 oz. (¼ cup) flour
2 tablespoons (3T) brandy (optional)
chopped fresh parsley to garnish

Season the chicken and fry in the heated oil in the open pressure cooker until lightly browned. Add the onion, garlic, mushrooms, tomatoes, wine, stock and herbs. Put on the lid, bring to HIGH (15 lb.) pressure and cook for 6-8 minutes, according to size of the joints.

Reduce pressure in cold water. Put the chicken and vegetables in a warm serving dish and keep hot. Discard the bay leaf. Mix the flour with a little cold water to form a smooth paste, then stir in a little of the hot stock. Add the mixture to the liquid in the cooker and bring it to the boil, stirring until the sauce thickens. Add brandy, if wished. Pour the sauce over the chicken and vegetables and sprinkle with parsley.
Serves 4

Florida Chicken Casserole

2½-3 lb. roasting chicken, thawed
  if frozen
1½ oz. (6T) flour
1 teaspoon paprika
1 teaspoon salt
freshly ground black pepper
1 oz. (2T) butter

1 orange, grated rind and juice
8 oz. can (1 cup) pineapple chunks
¼ pint (⅔ cup) chicken stock
2 teaspoons cornflour (cornstarch)
Garnish:
1 large orange, sliced

Joint the chicken into eight portions (breasts, thighs, drumsticks and wings) and remove the skin.

Put the flour, paprika, salt and a little black pepper in a paper bag and shake the portions in this mixture until they are well coated. Melt the butter in the open pressure cooker and fry the chicken portions until they are golden brown all over. Take the cooker from the heat and sprinkle the orange rind over the chicken. Make up the orange juice to ¼ pint (⅔ cup) with the juice from the pineapple. Pour over the chicken. Place the pineapple chunks on top. Add the stock. Put on the lid and bring to HIGH (15 lb.) pressure. Cook for 5 minutes.

Reduce pressure in cold water. Place the chicken in a warm casserole and spoon the pineapple over the top. Mix the cornflour to a smooth paste with a little cold water, stir in some of the hot cooking liquid, then add the mixture to the cooker. Bring to the boil, stirring, until the sauce has thickened, then pour it over the chicken. Serve with a green vegetable or green salad garnished with orange slices.
Serves 6-8

Chicken and Carrot Stew

4 chicken joints, thawed if frozen
2 large onions, sliced
2 oz. (¼ cup) butter
¾ lb. small whole carrots

¾ pint (2 cups) chicken stock
bouquet garni
salt and pepper
1 tablespoon flour

Lightly brown the chicken joints and onions in the melted butter in the open pressure cooker. Take the cooker off the heat and add the carrots and stock with the bouquet garni and seasoning. Put on the lid and bring to HIGH (15 lb.) pressure. Cook for 6-8 minutes, according to size of the joints.

Reduce pressure in cold water. Place the chicken joints and carrots in a warm casserole. Remove the bouquet garni. Mix the flour to a smooth paste with a little cold water, then mix in some of the hot stock. Return the cooker to the heat, add the flour mixture and bring to the boil, stirring, until the stock thickens. Pour the stock over the chicken and carrots.
Serves 4

FLORIDA CHICKEN CASSEROLE *(Photograph: Buxted Advisory Service)*

Boiled Chicken with Rice

1 boiling fowl weighing not more
  than 3 lb., thawed if frozen
1 lemon, juice and strips of peel
salt and pepper
1 onion, stuck with a clove
1 carrot, chopped
piece of turnip, chopped
2 celery stalks, chopped
1 leek, chopped

bouquet garni
6 peppercorns
8 oz. (1 ¼ cups) long grain rice
1 tablespoon flour
1 tablespoon chopped fresh
  parsley
Garnish:
lemon quarters
bacon rolls (see below)

Wipe and trim the chicken. Weigh it and calculate the cooking time, allowing 10 minutes per lb. Rub the chicken all over with lemon juice and season well. Put the chicken in the pressure cooker with enough water to half fill the base of the cooker. Bring to the boil and skim well. Tie the vegetables, lemon peel, herbs and peppercorns in a piece of muslin and put them in the cooker. Put on the lid and bring to HIGH (15 lb.) pressure.

Five minutes before the end of the calculated cooking time, reduce pressure in cold water. Return the cooker to the heat, uncovered, and reboil the liquid. Add the rice, put on the lid and bring to HIGH (15 lb.) pressure. Cook for a further 5 minutes, then allow the pressure to reduce at room temperature.

Remove the muslin bag of vegetables. Lift the chicken on to a warm serving dish and keep it hot. Strain the rice and arrange it round the chicken. Return the stock to the cooker. Mix the flour to a smooth paste with a little cold water. Mix in a little of the hot stock, then add the mixture to the cooker. Bring to the boil, stirring until the sauce thickens. Check the seasoning, stir in the parsley and serve the sauce separately. Garnish with lemon quarters and bacon rolls.

Serves 4
Bacon rolls:
Cut the rind off some bacon rashers (slices) and stretch them by running the back of a knife blade along them. Cut them in half, roll them up and secure with fine skewers. Grill all over until crisp.

Golden Harvest Casserole

Marinade:
1 tablespoon clear honey
1 tablespoon cider vinegar
1 tablespoon soy sauce
4 tablespoons (⅓ cup) dry cider

4 chicken joints, thawed if frozen
2 oz. (¼ cup) butter

2 onions, sliced
1 large green pepper, seeded and
 cut into strips
2 tablespoons (3T) flour
¼ pint (⅔ cup) dry cider
salt and pepper
15 oz. can peach halves, drained
chopped fresh parsley to garnish

The chicken in this recipe is marinaded for 12 hours, so start the preparation the day before, if necessary.

Mix the ingredients for the marinade. Put the chicken joints in a deep dish and pour the marinade over them. Leave for about 12 hours; turn the chicken now and again to ensure that it is coated all over with the marinade.

Drain the chicken joints from the marinade, but keep the liquid. Melt 1 oz (2T) of the butter in the open pressure cooker and fry the chicken until brown all over. Remove the chicken and drain. Then fry the onions and pepper for 1-2 minutes, drain them and take them out of the cooker. Melt the rest of the butter in the cooker and stir in the flour, cooking for 1 minute. Remove the cooked flour and set it aside.

Take the cooker off the heat and put in the chicken and vegetables. Pour in the cider and marinade, season, put on the lid and bring to HIGH (15 lb.) pressure. Cook for 5-7 minutes, according to the size of the joints.

Reduce pressure in cold water. Put the chicken joints in a warm casserole and keep hot. Return the cooker to the heat, add the cooked flour and bring to the boil, stirring until the sauce thickens. Add the peaches and heat through. Pour the sauce over the chicken and arrange the peach halves on top. Sprinkle with chopped parsley.
Serves 4

Poulet Henri IV

1 boiling fowl weighing not more
  than 3 lb., thawed if frozen
chicken stock
1 bay leaf
salt and pepper
1 lb. young carrots, scraped
1 lb. young turnips, peeled
1 lb. medium-sized potatoes,
  peeled and halved

1 small cabbage, trimmed and
  quartered
Sauce:
1 oz. (2T) butter
1 oz. (¼ cup) flour
1 garlic clove, crushed (optional)
2 tablespoons (3T) double
  (heavy) cream (optional)

Weigh the chicken and calculate the cooking time, allowing 10 minutes per lb.

Put the chicken in the cooker with enough stock to half fill the base and add the bay leaf and seasoning. Bring to the boil, uncovered, and skim well. Put on the lid and bring to HIGH (15 lb.) pressure.

Four minutes before the end of the calculated cooking time, reduce cooker pressure in cold water. Put in the carrots, turnips and potatoes then bring the liquid to the boil and add the cabbage. Put on the lid and bring to HIGH (15 lb.) pressure. Cook for a further 4 minutes.

Reduce the cooker pressure in cold water. Place the chicken on a warm serving dish and arrange the vegetables round it; keep hot. Strain the stock.

To make the sauce: melt the butter in a pan, stir in the flour and cook gently for 1 minute, then blend in 1 pint (2½ cups) of the stock. Add the garlic, if used. Bring to the boil, stirring all the time, and cook until the sauce thickens. Add salt and pepper and stir in the cream, if using, but do not reboil.

Serves 4

Note: If your pressure cooker is not large enough to hold the chicken and the vegetables together, cook the vegetables separately in the cooker while you are making the sauce. Put the trivet in the cooker and place the carrots, turnips and potatoes on it. Put the cabbage in a perforated separator. Sprinkle vegetables lightly with salt. Pour into the cooker ½ pint (1¼ cups) water, or stock if there is enough, and bring to the boil. Then put the cabbage in. Put on the lid and bring to HIGH (15 lb.) pressure, then cook for 4 minutes. Reduce pressure in cold water.

POULET HENRI IV (*Photograph: British Poultry Information Service*)

Coq au Vin

1 roasting chicken, jointed,
  thawed if frozen
2 oz. (¼ cup) butter
2 onions, sliced
2 tablespoons (3T) brandy
½ pint (1¼ cups) red wine

salt and pepper
1 garlic clove, crushed
bouquet garni
4 oz. bacon or uncooked ham,
  diced
4 oz. (1 cup) button mushrooms

Brown the chicken joints in the melted butter in the pressure cooker. Half way through browning, add the onions. Warm the brandy in a small pan, pour it over the chicken and set light to it. When the flames have died down, pour in the wine and add the seasoning, garlic and bouquet garni. Bring slowly to the boil. Meanwhile put the bacon in cold water in a small pan. Boil for a moment, then drain the bacon and put it in the cooker with the mushrooms. Put on the lid, bring to HIGH (15 lb.) pressure and cook for 6-8 minutes, according to size of the joints.

Reduce pressure in cold water. Arrange the chicken and mushrooms in a warm serving dish. Remove the bouquet garni. Boil the liquid rapidly in the open cooker until it has reduced and thickened. Then pour it over the chicken.
Serves 4

Chicken Béarnais

2 oz. (¼ cup) butter
4 chicken joints
2 onions, sliced
4 oz. (½ cup) bacon, diced
3 carrots, sliced
⅓ pint (1 cup) white wine or stock

3-4 tomatoes, skinned and sliced
salt
freshly ground black pepper
¼ teaspoon dried thyme
chopped fresh parsley to garnish

Heat the butter in the open pressure cooker and sauté the chicken joints until golden brown on all sides. Take out and drain off excess fat.

Add the onions and bacon to the pressure cooker and fry gently until just tender. Add the sliced carrots and arrange the chicken joints on top. Pour over the wine or stock and add the tomatoes. Season with salt and pepper and sprinkle with the thyme.

Put the lid on the pressure cooker, bring to HIGH (15 lb.) pressure and cook for 7 minutes. Reduce the pressure in cold water.

Arrange the chicken joints on a serving dish, spoon the cooking liquor over and top with the vegetables. Sprinkle with chopped parsley to garnish.
Serves 4

For a richer flavour, pour 2 tablespoons (3T) double (heavy) cream over the chicken before serving.

Chicken Curry

2 oz. (¼ cup) butter or margarine
4 chicken joints
2 onions, sliced
2 cloves garlic, crushed
3-4 teaspoons curry powder
1 pint (2½ cups) chicken stock
juice of ½ lemon

1-2 teaspoons salt
¼ teaspoon freshly ground black
 pepper
4 bay leaves
4 sticks cinnamon (optional)
7 oz. (1 cup) rice
¾ pint (2 cups) salted water

Heat the butter or margarine in the open pressure cooker and fry the chicken joints until golden brown on all sides. Take out of the cooker and set aside.

Add the onions and garlic to the fat remaining in the cooker and sauté over low heat; do not allow them to brown. When the onions are just tender stir in the curry powder and cook, stirring constantly, for 1 minute.

Pour in the stock and lemon juice. Replace the chicken joints in the pressure cooker. Add the salt, pepper, bay leaves and cinnamon sticks, if used. Bring to the boil in the open pressure cooker then put on the lid and bring to HIGH (15 lb.) pressure. Cook for 7 minutes then reduce pressure in cold water.

Remove the lid from the pressure cooker and put in the trivet. Put the rice and salted water in a basin, cover and place on the trivet. Put the lid on the pressure cooker and bring to HIGH (15 lb.) pressure. Cook for 5 minutes. Allow pressure to reduce at room temperature.

Lift out the rice, toss to separate the grains and turn into an ovenproof serving dish. Leave in a warm oven for a few minutes to dry off.

Taste the curry and adjust the seasoning if necessary. Pour into a dish and serve the rice separately. Grated coconut, diced cucumber, tomato and onion salad and a bowl of plain yogurt are suitable side dishes to accompany this curry.

Serves 4

Chicken Basquaise

6 chicken joints, thawed if frozen
1 tablespoon oil
1 oz. (2T) butter
1 medium-sized onion, sliced
1 garlic clove, crushed
1 green pepper, seeded and sliced
small can pimento (pimiento),
   sliced

1 tablespoon flour
¼ pint (⅔ cup) chicken stock
½ pint (1¼ cups) white wine
salt and pepper
2 teaspoons tomato purée
1 teaspoon paprika
sprig of fresh parsley to garnish

Fry the chicken joints in the oil and butter in the open pressure cooker until golden brown all over, then take out of the cooker. Add the onion, garlic , pepper and pimento and cook until softened, then remove from the cooker. Sprinkle the flour in the remaining fat and cook for a minute or two, then set it aside. Return chicken and vegetables to the cooker. Add the stock, wine, seasoning, tomato purée and paprika. Put on the lid, bring to HIGH (15 lb.) pressure and cook for 7 minutes. Reduce pressure in cold water. Return the open cooker to the heat, add the cooked flour and bring to the boil, stirring until the sauce has thickened. Garnish with a sprig of parsley. Serve with boiled rice.
Serves 6

Duck and Cherry Casserole

4 duck joints
4 tablespoons (⅓ cup) oil
1 onion, sliced
8 oz. can cherries

brown stock
3 tablespoons (¼ cup) cranberry
   sauce or jelly
salt and pepper

Fry the duck joints in oil in the open pressure cooker until golden brown all over. Take the duck joints out and fry the onion until soft and golden. Drain off excess fat and return the duck joints to the cooker. Drain the cherries and make up the juice to ¾ pint (2 cups) with stock. Pour the liquid into the cooker, add the cranberry sauce or jelly and season. Put on the lid and bring to HIGH (15 lb.) pressure. Cook for 12 minutes.

Reduce pressure in cold water. Arrange the duck joints in a warm casserole and keep hot. Thicken the liquid if necessary. To do this, mix 1 tablespoon flour with a little cold water and stir in some of the hot liquid. Add the mixture to the cooker and bring the sauce to the boil, stirring until it thickens. Add the cherries and heat through. Pour the sauce over the duck.
Serves 4

CHICKEN BASQUAISE *(Photograph: British Poultry Information Service)*

Venison Casserole

1 lb. stewing venison, cubed
seasoned flour for coating
2 tablespoons (3T) oil
1 onion, sliced
½ pint (1¼ cups) brown stock

¼ pint (⅔ cup) red wine
1 tablespoon redcurrant jelly
½ orange, juice and grated rind
½ lb. medium-sized potatoes,
 halved

Toss the venison in seasoned flour and fry it in the oil in the open pressure cooker until it is lightly browned. Add the onion and continue cooking until the onion is softened. Take the cooker off the heat and add the stock and red wine, mixed with the redcurrant jelly, orange juice and rind. Put on the lid and bring to HIGH (15 lb.) pressure. Cook for 20-25 minutes, depending on age of the meat.

Four minutes before the end of the cooking time, reduce pressure in cold water and add the potatoes. Put on the lid, bring to HIGH (15 lb.) pressure and continue cooking for 4 minutes. Reduce pressure in cold water. Transfer the venison and potatoes to a warm serving dish. Adjust seasoning and rapidly boil the liquid in the open cooker until it is reduced and thickened, then pour it over the venison.
Serves 4

Hunter's Casserole

1 onion, chopped
4 oz. bacon (ham), diced
3 tablespoons (¼ cup) oil
4 wood pigeons
¼ pint (⅔ cup) red wine

½ pint (1¼ cups) brown stock
salt and pepper
3 carrots, sliced
¼ lb. (1 cup) button mushrooms

Fry the onion and bacon in the oil in the open pressure cooker for 2 minutes, then add the pigeons and fry until they are browned all over. Take the cooker off the heat and add the wine, stock and seasoning. Put in the carrots and mushrooms. Put on the lid and bring to HIGH (15 lb.) pressure. Cook for 10-12 minutes, depending on the age of the birds.

Reduce pressure in cold water. Arrange the pigeons and vegetables on a warm serving dish and keep hot. Boil the sauce rapidly in the open cooker until it is reduced and thickened. Pour the sauce over the pigeons and vegetables.
Serves 4

Rich Rabbit Stew

4 rabbit joints
seasoned flour for coating
2 tablespoons (3T) oil
1 oz. (2T) butter
1 onion, sliced

¾ pint (2 cups) brown stock
1 tablespoon tomato purée
8 oz. can small frankfurter
  sausages
chopped fresh parsley to garnish

Toss the rabbit joints in seasoned flour and fry them in the oil and butter in the open pressure cooker until lightly browned all over. Add the onion and continue frying until the onion is soft and golden. Take the cooker off the heat and pour in the stock mixed with the tomato purée. Put on the lid and bring to HIGH (15 lb.) pressure. Cook for 15 minutes.

Reduce pressure in cold water. Drain the frankfurters and add them to the cooker. Continue to cook, uncovered, until the liquid has reduced and thickened and the frankfurters are heated through. Sprinkle with chopped parsley and serve with creamed potatoes.

Serves 4

Rabbit in Mustard Sauce

2½ lb. rabbit
4 tablespoons (⅓ cup) French
  mustard
salt and pepper
1 oz. (¼ cup) flour
1 oz. (2T) butter
3 slices streaky (fatty) bacon, diced

2 large onions, sliced
½ pint (1¼ cups) chicken stock
piece of lemon rind
bouquet garni
3 tablespoons (¼ cup) double
  (heavy) cream
chopped fresh parsley to garnish

Clean and dry the rabbit thoroughly then cut into four joints. Spread each joint evenly with mustard, cover and leave for 1-2 hours.

Season the rabbit joints with salt and pepper and toss in flour to coat evenly. Melt the butter in the open pressure cooker and fry the rabbit until evenly browned. Take out of the pressure cooker.

Heat the bacon gently in the open cooker until the fat runs. Add the onions and sauté until just softened. Return the rabbit joints to the cooker. Add the stock, lemon rind and bouquet garni.

Put the lid on the pressure cooker, bring to HIGH (15 lb.) pressure and cook for 20-25 minutes. Reduce pressure at room temperature. Remove the bouquet garni and lemon rind and adjust the seasoning, if necessary. Transfer the rabbit joints to a warm serving dish.

Boil the liquid in the open pressure cooker until reduced by about half. Lower the heat and add the cream, stirring until well blended. Pour the sauce over the rabbit and garnish with chopped parsley.

Serves 4

Jugged Rabbit

4 rabbit joints
seasoned flour for coating
1 oz. (2T) butter
4 oz. streaky (fatty) bacon slices,
  cut into ½ inch pieces
½ lb. button onions

½ pint (1¼ cups) brown stock
¼ pint (⅔ cup) red wine
2 tablespoons (3T) redcurrant jelly
1 teaspoon mixed dried herbs
forcemeat balls (see below)

Toss the rabbit joints in seasoned flour and fry in the butter in the open pressure cooker until lightly browned. Take the joints out of the cooker. Fry the bacon and onions in the remaining fat in the cooker until the onions are golden. Take the cooker off the heat and pour in the stock and the wine mixed with the redcurrant jelly. Add the herbs. Put on the lid, bring to HIGH (15 lb.) pressure and cook for 15 minutes.

Reduce pressure in cold water. Put the rabbit and onions in a warm casserole. Boil the liquid rapidly in the open cooker until it has reduced and thickened, adjust seasoning and pour the sauce over the rabbit. Add the forcemeat balls.
Serves 4

Forcemeat Balls

2 oz. (1 cup) fresh breadcrumbs
1 oz. (2½T) shredded suet
salt and pepper
2 tablespoons (3T) chopped
  mixed herbs

1 small egg, beaten
oil for deep frying

Mix the crumbs and suet together, season well, add the herbs and enough beaten egg to bind. Roll the mixture into small balls and fry them in the hot oil until golden.

JUGGED RABBIT *(Photograph: Bisto)*

MEAT

Paprika Pork

1 lb. lean pork
seasoned flour
1 oz. (2T) lard (shortening)
1 large onion, sliced
1 tablespoon paprika

½ pint (1¼ cups) chicken stock
15 oz. can tomatoes
1 teaspoon sugar
1 bay leaf
½ lb. (1½ cups) frozen peas

Trim excess fat from the meat and cut into cubes or thin slices. Coat the meat in seasoned flour and fry it lightly in the lard in the open pressure cooker with the onion. Stir in the paprika and all the remaining ingredients except the peas. Stir until the liquid boils. Then put on the lid, bring to HIGH (15 lb.) pressure and cook for 25 minutes.

Reduce pressure at room temperature, bring back to the boil and add the frozen peas. Cook in the open pressure cooker for 5 minutes. Remove the bay leaf and thicken if necessary with 1 tablespoon flour mixed with a little cold water.
Serves 4

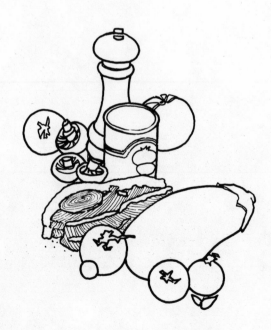

Pork and Prune Casserole

8 oz. (1⅓ cups) dried prunes
2 lb. pork rib chops
2 tablespoons (3T) oil
¼ pint (⅔ cup) apple juice

¼ pint (⅔ cup) water
salt and pepper
1 tablespoon flour

Pour boiling water over the prunes and leave to soak for 10 minutes.
Remove excess fat from the pork. Fry the meat in the oil in the open
pressure cooker until browned. Take cooker off heat and drain off excess
fat. Add the drained prunes, the apple juice, water and seasoning. Put on
the lid and bring to HIGH (15 lb.) pressure. Cook for 10-12 minutes,
according to thickness of the chops.

Reduce pressure in cold water. Arrange the chops and prunes in a warm
serving dish. Mix the flour to a smooth paste with a little cold water, add
some of the hot liquid and stir it into the cooker. Bring to the boil, stirring,
until the sauce thickens, then pour it over the chops.
Serves 4-6

Bacon in Cider

2½ lb. bacon collar joint (smoked
  picnic shoulder of pork)
½ pint (1¼ cups) cider
¼ pint (⅔ cup) water
1 small onion, quartered

1 carrot, quartered
1 bay leaf
6 peppercorns
2 oz. (½ cup) toasted
  breadcrumbs

Put the joint in the pressure cooker and cover with cold water. Bring the
water to the boil, uncovered, then remove the meat and discard the water.

Put the trivet in the cooker, replace the meat in the cooker, pour on the
cider and water and add the vegetables, bay leaf and peppercorns. Put on
the lid, bring to HIGH (15 lb.) pressure and cook for 30 minutes.

Reduce pressure at room temperature. Leave the joint to cool in the
liquid, then strip off the rind. Press the browned breadcrumbs over the
surface. Serve cold.

Use the cooking liquid as stock for another dish or for a sauce.
Serves 4-6

Bacon with Pineapple Sauce

2½ lb. bacon collar joint (smoked picnic shoulder of pork), rolled
flavouring vegetables (optional)
bouquet garni
6 peppercorns
Sauce:
1 tablespoon cornflour (cornstarch)

8½ oz. can crushed pineapple
4 tablespoons (⅓ cup) demerara sugar
pinch of ground ginger
2 teaspoons white vinegar
1 tablespoon tomato ketchup (catsup)

Put the bacon joint in the pressure cooker and cover with cold water. Bring the water to the boil, uncovered, then remove the meat and discard the water. Put the trivet in the cooker, replace the meat, pour on ¾ pint (2 cups) water and add flavouring vegetables, if required, bouquet garni and peppercorns. Put on the lid, bring to HIGH (15 lb.) pressure and cook for 30 minutes.

Reduce pressure at room temperature. Meanwhile make the sauce. Blend the cornflour to a smooth paste with a little cold water and put it in a pan with the remaining ingredients. Heat gently to dissolve the sugar and cook, stirring, until the sauce thickens and clears.

Remove the joint from the cooker. When it is cool enough to handle, strip off the rind and spread some of the sauce on top. Serve hot and pass the rest of the sauce separately. New potatoes and buttered sweetcorn go well with this dish.

Serves 4-6

BACON WITH PINEAPPLE SAUCE *(Photograph: Danish Food Centre)*

Bacon with Barbecue Relish

3 lb. bacon collar joint (smoked
 picnic shoulder of pork)
1 onion, sliced
1 bay leaf
few peppercorns
demerara sugar for coating
Barbecue relish:
1 oz. (2T) butter

1 onion, finely chopped
14 oz. can tomatoes
2 tablespoons (3T) cider vinegar
2 tablespoons (3T) demerara
 sugar
dash of Worcestershire sauce
2 tablespoons (3T) sweet pickle
½ teaspoon French mustard

Put the joint in the pressure cooker with water to cover and bring to the
boil. Remove the joint and discard the water. Put the trivet in the cooker,
replace the joint and pour in ¾ pint (2 cups) water. Add the onion, bay leaf
and peppercorns. Put on the lid and bring to HIGH (15 lb.) pressure. Cook
for 36 minutes.

Reduce pressure at room temperature. Lift out the joint and when it is
cool enough to handle, strip off the rind. Score the fat in a criss-cross
pattern and coat it with sugar. Crisp off in the centre of the oven at 400°F,
Gas Mark 6, for about 10 minutes.

To make the barbecue relish, melt the butter in a pan, add the chopped
onion and cook until soft, without browning, for 5 minutes. Add remaining
ingredients, bring to the boil, reduce heat and simmer for 10 minutes.
Serve hot or cold.

Serve the meat with the relish.
Serves 6

Bacon Stewpot

1 ½ lb. bacon collar joint (smoked
  picnic shoulder of pork)
1 ½ oz. (3T) butter
½ lb. leeks, washed, trimmed and
  sliced
1 small onion, chopped

2 carrots, sliced
1 pint (2 ½ cups) stock
pepper
1 tablespoon flour
7 ½ oz. can butter beans
1 tablespoon chopped parsley

Remove rind and excess fat from the bacon and cut the meat into 1 inch
cubes. Put the meat in the pressure cooker, cover it with cold water and
bring to the boil. Strain off the water and drain the meat on absorbent
kitchen paper. Rinse and dry the cooker.

Melt the butter in the open cooker and gently cook the leeks and onion
until soft but not brown. Remove the cooker from the heat and add the
carrots, meat, stock and pepper. Put on the lid, bring to HIGH (15 lb.)
pressure and cook for 20 minutes.

Reduce pressure at room temperature. Mix the flour with a little cold
water, stir in some of the hot liquid and add the mixture to the cooker.
Bring to the boil, uncovered, and stir until the liquid thickens. Lower the
heat and add the drained beans and parsley. Heat through for about 5
minutes. Serve with peas and creamed potatoes.

Serves 4

Lamb and Apricot Stew

1 ½ lb. lean lamb, cubed
seasoned flour
3 tablespoons (¼ cup) oil
1 onion, chopped

1 pint (2 ½ cups) stock
bouquet garni
6 oz. (1 cup) dried apricots
few split almonds

Coat the lamb in seasoned flour. Heat the oil in the open pressure cooker
and fry the onion gently for 3 minutes. Add the lamb to the cooker and fry
until it is lightly browned. Take the cooker off the heat and add the stock
and bouquet garni. Put on the lid and bring to HIGH (15 lb.) pressure.
Cook for 10 minutes.

Meanwhile, pour boiling water over the apricots and leave to soak for 10
minutes. Reduce cooker pressure in cold water and add the drained
apricots. Put on the lid and bring to HIGH (15 lb.) pressure. Cook for a
further 3 minutes and reduce pressure at room temperature. Remove the
bouquet garni and scatter the almonds over the stew before serving.

Serves 4-6

Midsummer Lamb

1 oz. (2T) butter
1 onion, sliced
½ lb. carrots, sliced
1 medium-sized turnip, diced
1 lb. boned leg or shoulder of
  lamb, cubed
¼ lb. (1 cup) button mushrooms,
  halved

¼ pint (⅔ cup) dry cider
½ pint (1 ¼ cups) stock
pinch of dried marjoram
salt and pepper
1 oz. (¼ cup) flour
2 tablespoons (3T) single (light)
  cream
chopped fresh parsley to garnish

Melt the butter in the open pressure cooker and gently cook the onion, carrots and turnip for 2-3 minutes. Add the lamb and mushrooms and cook for a further minute. Remove the cooker from the heat and add the cider and stock with the marjoram and seasoning. Put on the lid and bring to HIGH (15 lb.) pressure. Cook for 12 minutes.

Reduce pressure in cold water. Mix the flour to a smooth paste with a little cold water and stir in some of the hot liquid. Return the open cooker to the heat, stir in the flour mixture and bring to the boil, stirring, until the liquid thickens. Just before serving, stir in the cream and sprinkle with parsley.

Serves 4

Navarin of Lamb

2 lb. stewing lamb, chopped
2 oz. (¼ cup) butter
2 onions, quartered
¾ pint (2 cups) stock
2 lb. turnips, diced

2 carrots, sliced
bouquet garni
salt and pepper
1 tablespoon flour

Brown the meat in the melted butter in the open pressure cooker with the onions. Remove the cooker from the heat and add the stock, vegetables, bouquet garni and seasoning. Put on the lid and bring to HIGH (15 lb.) pressure. Cook for 12 minutes.

Reduce pressure in cold water. Discard the bouquet garni. Mix the flour to a smooth paste with a little cold water, add some of the hot stock and stir the mixture into the contents of the cooker. Put the open cooker back on the heat and bring to the boil, stirring until the liquid thickens. Serve the meat surrounded by the vegetables.

Serves 4

Lamb Stew with Onion Dumplings

3 lb. middle neck of lamb cutlets
  (rib chops)
1 oz. (2T) dripping
2 onions, sliced
3 large carrots, sliced
2 turnips, sliced
¾ pint (2 cups) stock
1 teaspoon dried thyme
1 tablespoon chopped fresh
  parsley

salt and pepper
Onion dumplings:
2 oz. (¼ cup) butter
1 large onion, finely chopped
4 oz. (2 cups) fresh white
  breadcrumbs
2 oz. (½ cup) self-raising flour
½ teaspoon salt
pepper
1 egg, beaten

Fry the meat in the melted dripping in the open pressure cooker until it is browned all over. Remove meat and add the onions and cook gently for 5 minutes. Add the carrots and turnips and cook for a further 3 minutes. Take the cooker off the heat and pour in the stock. Add the thyme, parsley and seasoning. Put on the lid, bring to HIGH (15 lb.) pressure and cook for 10 minutes.

To make the dumplings, melt the butter in a pan and cook the onion gently for 5 minutes until soft but not coloured. Add the onion and butter to the breadcrumbs, flour, salt and pepper. Mix and bind with the egg. Shape the mixture into eight balls.

Reduce cooker pressure in cold water. Return the cooker to heat and bring to the boil, uncovered. Drop in the dumplings and place a plate over the cooker. Simmer for 10 minutes.
Serves 4

Beef Olives

Stuffing:
3 oz. (1 ½ cups) fresh white
  breadcrumbs
3 oz. (⅓ cup) cooked ham,
  chopped
1 tablespoon chopped fresh
  parsley
½ teaspoon mixed dried herbs
grated rind of ½ lemon
salt and pepper
1 ½ oz. (3T) melted butter
beaten egg to bind

4 slices beef topside (top round
  steak)
seasoned flour
2 onions, sliced
3 tablespoons (¼ cup) oil
½ pint (1 ¼ cups) brown stock
1 bay leaf

Combine all the stuffing ingredients, using just enough egg to bind. Batten out the meat and spread the stuffing over it. Roll up into small parcels and tie with string. Toss the rolled meat in seasoned flour.

   Brown the meat and onions in the oil in the open pressure cooker. Remove the cooker from the heat and add the stock and bay leaf. Put on the lid and bring to HIGH (15 lb.) pressure. Cook for 20 minutes. Reduce pressure in cold water. Remove the string and bay leaf before serving.
Serves 4

Old Fashioned Steak and Kidney Casserole

1 ¾ lb. stewing steak, cubed
6 oz. ox kidney, cored and
  chopped
2 tablespoons (3T) flour
1 onion, sliced
2 oz. (¼ cup) butter

1 pint (2½ cups) brown stock
1 teaspoon mixed dried herbs
salt and pepper
4 oz. shelled mussels (fresh or in
  brine)

Toss the beef and kidney in the flour. Fry the onion in the melted butter in the open pressure cooker until soft, then add the meat and brown all over. Drain off any excess fat and add the stock, herbs and seasoning. Put on the lid, bring to HIGH (15 lb.) pressure and cook for 15-20 minutes, according to quality of the meat.

Reduce pressure in cold water. Put the open cooker back on the heat, add the mussels (drained if in brine) and cover the cooker with a plate. Simmer for 10-15 minutes. Serve with peas or runner beans and potatoes.
Serves 4-6

Beef Pot Roast

½ lb. button onions
½ lb. carrots, cut into 2 inch
  lengths
2 celery stalks, cut into ½ inch
  lengths

2 oz. (¼ cup) butter
3 lb. boned and rolled brisket of
  beef
1 pint (2½ cups) brown stock
salt and pepper

Fry the vegetables in the butter in the open pressure cooker for 5 minutes. Take them out of the cooker and brown the meat all over in the remaining fat. Remove the cooker from the heat and add the vegetables, stock and seasoning. Put on the lid and bring to HIGH (15 lb.) pressure. Cook for 36-45 minutes, depending on the thickness of the meat (allowing 12-15 minutes per lb.). Reduce pressure at room temperature.

Arrange the meat on a warm serving dish with the vegetables surrounding it. If you wish to make gravy with the stock, thicken it with 1 tablespoon of flour mixed with cold water and darken with a little gravy browning if necessary.
Serves 6

OLD FASHIONED STEAK AND KIDNEY CASSEROLE
(Photograph: Bisto)

Steak and Kidney Pudding

Pastry:
8 oz. (2 cups) self-raising flour
4 oz. (½ cup) shredded suet
salt and pepper
water to mix

¾ lb. stewing steak, cubed
2-3 lambs' kidneys, cored and
  diced
2 tablespoons (3T) flour
brown stock or water

Mix the pastry ingredients with enough water to give a stiff dough. Roll out two thirds of the dough and line a greased 2 pint (5 cup) pudding basin (mold). Arrange the steak and kidney in layers in the basin, sprinkling each layer with seasoned flour. Pour in enough stock to come three-quarters of the way up the pudding. Roll out the remaining dough to form a lid, moisten the edges and seal together well. Cover with foil or greased greaseproof (waxed) paper and tie down with string, making a handle to go over the top.

Put the trivet in the pressure cooker and pour in 1½ pints (3¾ cups) boiling water and a little vinegar to prevent discoloration of the cooker. Put the pudding on the trivet. Put on the lid and lower the heat so that there is a gentle but steady flow of steam. Let it steam for 15 minutes without the weight, then increase the heat to bring to LOW (5 lb.) pressure. Cook for 55 minutes. Reduce pressure at room temperature.
Serves 4-6

Oxtail Stew

1 oxtail, jointed
seasoned flour for coating
3 bacon rashers (slices), chopped
2 onions, sliced

2 tablespoons (3T) oil
1¼ pints (3 cups) brown stock
1 teaspoon dried mixed herbs

Trim excess fat from the oxtail and toss in the seasoned flour. Fry the bacon and onions in the oil in the open cooker, then take them out. Fry the oxtail until it is brown all over. Drain off excess fat and add the stock and herbs. Put on the lid and bring to HIGH (15 lb.) pressure. Cook for 40 minutes. Reduce pressure at room temperature. Leave it to get cold, then remove the fat and pressure cook for a further 5 minutes before serving.
Serves 4-6

Boiled Beef and Dumplings

joint of salted silverside weighing
  not more than 3 lb.
bouquet garni
1 lb. carrots
2 onions
1 large turnip

Dumplings:
8 oz. self-raising flour
pinch of salt
4 oz. (½ cup) shredded suet
water to mix

Trim, wipe and weigh the meat and put it in the pressure cooker. Cover with water, bring to the boil, remove the meat and discard the water. Return the joint to the cooker and add enough water to half fill the cooker. Add the bouquet garni. Put on the lid and bring to HIGH (15 lb.) pressure. Allow 15 minutes per lb. cooking time. Meanwhile cut the vegetables into even-sized pieces.

Reduce pressure in cold water 5 minutes before the end of the cooking time. Put the vegetables in the cooker, bring to HIGH (15 lb.) pressure and cook for a further 5 minutes.

Mix together the dry ingredients for the dumplings and add enough water to make a stiff dough. Divide the dough into eight balls with well-floured hands. Reduce cooker pressure in cold water and return the cooker to the heat. Bring the liquid to the boil and drop in the dumplings. Cover with a plate and boil gently for 10 minutes. Discard the bouquet garni. Put the meat on a warm serving dish, surround with the vegetables and dumplings. Pour over some of the cooking liquid and serve the rest separately.
Serves 8

Kidney and Mushroom Pudding

Pastry:
6 oz. (1½ cups) self-raising flour
3 oz. (⅜ cup) shredded suet
salt and pepper
water to mix

¾ lb. lambs' kidneys, cored and
  diced
1 tablespoon flour
7½ oz. can small mushrooms,
  drained, reserving brine

Mix the pastry ingredients with enough water to make a stiff dough. Roll out two-thirds of the dough and line a greased 1½ pint (3¾ cup) pudding basin (mold). Toss the kidneys in seasoned flour and pack with the mushrooms into the lined basin. Pour in sufficient brine to come three-quarters of the way up the pudding. Roll out the remaining dough to form a lid, moisten the edges and seal the pastry well. Cover with foil or greased greaseproof (waxed) paper and tie down with string, making a handle to go over the top.

Put the trivet in the pressure cooker and put in 1½ pints (3¾ cups) boiling water and a little vinegar to prevent discoloration of the cooker. Put the pudding on the trivet. Put on the lid and lower the heat so that there is a gentle but steady flow of steam. Let it steam for 10 minutes without the weight, then increase the heat to bring to LOW (5 lb.) pressure. Cook for 25 minutes. Reduce pressure at room temperature.

Serves 4

Carbonnade of Beef

1½ lb. lean stewing beef, cut into
  strips
flour for coating
2 onions, sliced
2 oz. (¼ cup) butter

½ pint (1¼ cups) beer
¼ pint (⅔ cup) brown stock
salt and pepper
2 teaspoons made mustard
2 teaspoons sugar

Toss the beef strips in flour. Fry the onion in the fat in the open pressure cooker for 4 minutes, then add the meat and fry it until brown on both sides. Take the cooker off the heat and pour in the beer and stock. Add the seasoning, mustard and sugar. Put on the lid and bring to HIGH (15 lb.) pressure. Cook for 15-20 minutes, depending on the thickness and tenderness of the beef. Serve with boiled rice, noodles or jacket potatoes.

Serves 4-6

KIDNEY AND MUSHROOM PUDDING *(Photograph: Chesswood Mushrooms)*

Stuffed Savoury Hearts

3 tablespoons (¼ cup) sage and
  onion stuffing mix
5 tablespoons (6T) boiling water
4 lambs' hearts
seasoned flour for coating
3 tablespoons (¼ cup) oil

1 onion, sliced
¼ lb. carrots, sliced
4 celery stalks, chopped
2 teaspoons mixed dried herbs
1 pint (2½ cups) brown stock

Put the stuffing mix in a bowl. Add the boiling water, stir and leave it to stand. Wash the hearts, remove the tubes, gristle and fat, then wash and dry. Cut through the centre dividing tissue to make room for the stuffing. Stuff the hearts and tie with string. Coat them in seasoned flour and fry in oil in the open pressure cooker until brown all over. Then take them out and fry the vegetables lightly in the remaining oil.

    Return the hearts to the cooker with the herbs and stock. Put on the lid and bring to HIGH (15 lb.) pressure. Cook for 30 minutes. Reduce pressure in cold water.

Serves 4

Moroccan Chick Pea Stew

6 oz. (¾ cup) chick peas
1½ lb. middle neck of lamb cutlets
  (rib chops)
seasoned flour for coating
3 tablespoons (¼ cup) oil
1 onion, sliced
½ teaspoon ground (powdered)
  ginger

½ teaspoon mixed spice
¾ pint (2 cups) stock
1 aubergine (eggplant), chopped
  and salted
1 green pepper, seeded and
  chopped
3 tomatoes, quartered

Soak the chick peas for 1 hour in cold water. Trim excess fat off the lamb and toss it in the seasoned flour. Heat the oil in the open pressure cooker and fry the lamb and onion until lightly browned. Stir in the spices and gradually add the stock. Rinse the chopped aubergine and drain thoroughly. Bring to the boil and add the drained chick peas, aubergine, green pepper and tomatoes. Put on the lid and bring to HIGH (15 lb.) pressure. Cook for 15 minutes. Reduce pressure at room temperature.
Serves 4-6

Chilli con Carne

8 oz. (1⅓ cups) red kidney beans
2 tablespoons (3T) oil
1 lb. minced (ground) beef
1 large onion, chopped
8 oz. can tomatoes

salt and pepper
1 tablespoon vinegar
1 tablespoon sugar
1-2 teaspoons chilli powder

Pour boiling water over the beans and leave them to soak for 1 hour. Heat the oil in the open pressure cooker and quickly fry the meat until brown. Add the onion and cook for a little longer.

Strain the beans and the tomatoes, reserving the tomato juice. Add the beans and tomatoes to the meat and onion. Add enough water to the tomato juice to make ¾ pint (2 cups) and pour it over the meat. Add the salt, pepper, vinegar and sugar. Add 1-2 teaspoons chilli powder according to strength. Put on the lid and bring to HIGH (15 lb.) pressure. Cook for 15 minutes and reduce pressure at room temperature. If necessary, cook in the open pan to reduce liquid.
Serves 4

Lamb and Bean Hotpot

4 oz. (½ cup) haricot (navy) beans
4 oz. (⅔ cup) red kidney beans
4 pieces scrag neck of lamb
2 tablespoons (3T) oil

1 onion, sliced
salt and pepper
bouquet garni
¾ pint (2 cups) brown stock

Pour boiling water over the beans and leave them to soak for 1 hour. Trim excess fat from the lamb and brown it in the oil in the open pressure cooker. Drain off excess fat. Drain the beans and put them in the cooker with the meat, sliced onion, seasoning and bouquet garni. Pour in the stock. Put on the lid and bring to HIGH (15 lb.) pressure. Cook for 20 minutes. Reduce pressure in cold water. Remove the bouquet garni before serving.
Serves 4

Cassoulet

6 oz. (1 cup) butter beans
½ lb. breast of lamb
¾ lb. boned blade of pork
6 oz. garlic-flavoured boiling
  sausage, sliced
1½ oz. (3T) butter

4 oz. salt pork or streaky (fatty)
  bacon, chopped
2 onions, sliced
bouquet garni
salt and pepper
1 pint (2½ cups) water

Pour boiling water over the beans and leave to soak for 1 hour. Trim the fat from the lamb and pork and cut it into cubes. Fry the lamb, pork and sausage in the butter in the open pressure cooker. Drain off excess fat and add the drained beans, salt pork, onions, bouquet garni and seasoning. Pour in the water. Put on the lid and bring to HIGH (15 lb.) pressure. Cook for 30 minutes. Reduce pressure at room temperature. Discard the bouquet garni.
Serves 6

LAMB AND BEAN HOTPOT *(Photograph: Bisto)*

VEGETABLES

Casseroled Cabbage Leaves

1 medium-sized cabbage
1 teaspoon cornflour (cornstarch)
¼ pint (⅔ cup) stock
8 oz. can tomatoes
Stuffing:
¾ lb. pork sausage meat
2 oz. (1 cup) fresh breadcrumbs

½ onion, finely chopped
grated rind of ½ lemon
2 tablespoons (3T) chopped fresh
 parsley
1 tablespoon chopped mint
1 teaspoon mixed dried herbs
salt and pepper

Blanch the cabbage in boiling water for a few minutes. Drain it and discard
any damaged leaves. Select 12 good leaves. Mix together the stuffing
ingredients. Divide the stuffing between the leaves and roll each one into a
parcel. Put the cabbage parcels in a heatproof dish or casserole which will
fit easily into the pressure cooker. Mix the cornflour to a smooth paste with
a little cold water, then blend it with the stock. Mix the stock with the
tomatoes and their juice and pour the mixture over the cabbage leaves.
Season lightly. Cover the dish with foil.

   Put the trivet in the cooker with ½ pint (1¼ cups) water. Stand the dish
on the trivet, put on the lid and bring to HIGH (15 lb.) pressure. Cook for
8-10 minutes, depending on the thickness of the dish. Reduce pressure in
cold water.
Serves 4-6

Spicy Red Cabbage

1 small or ½ large red cabbage
1 oz. (2T) butter
1 small onion, chopped
1 cooking apple, peeled, cored
 and sliced

2 tablespoons (3T) wine vinegar
2 tablespoons (3T) water
1 tablespoon brown sugar
salt and pepper

Cut the cabbage into quarters, discard the core, and shred finely. Heat the
butter in the open pressure cooker and fry the onion lightly. Add the
cabbage, apple, vinegar, water, sugar and seasoning. Put on the lid and
bring to HIGH (15 lb.) pressure. Cook for 4 minutes and reduce pressure
in cold water.
Serves 4-6

Pease Pudding

1 lb. (2 cups) yellow split peas
1 pint (2½ cups) water, ham or
  bacon stock

1 large egg, beaten
large knob of butter
salt and pepper

Pour boiling water over the peas and leave them to soak for 1 hour. Put the water or stock and the soaked peas in the pressure cooker and bring to the boil uncovered. Remove the scum and lower the heat so that the liquid is boiling gently but not rising in the pan. Put on the lid and bring to HIGH (15 lb.) pressure without altering the heat. Then cook for 8 minutes.

Reduce pressure at room temperature. Strain the peas and mash them with the beaten egg, butter and seasoning. Put the mixture in a greased bowl, cover with buttered greaseproof (waxed) paper and tie securely. Rinse the cooker, put in the trivet and ½ pint (1¼ cups) water. Stand the bowl on the trivet. Put on the lid and bring to HIGH (15 lb.) pressure. Cook for 4 minutes. Reduce pressure at room temperature. Turn the pease pudding out and cut it into slices. Serve with boiled ham or other meats.
Serves 4

Lentils à la Dijonnaise

8 oz. (1 cup) lentils
2 onions
bouquet garni
salt
3 oz. ham
1 oz. (2T) butter

1 tablespoon flour
½ pint (1¼ cups) stock
pepper
½ teaspoon strong mustard
1 teaspoon chopped fresh parsley

Wash the lentils and put them in the pressure cooker with 1 pint (2½ cups) water. Bring to the boil uncovered and remove the scum. Add 1 onion, halved, the herbs and a little salt. Put on the lid and bring to HIGH (15 lb.) pressure. Cook for 15 minutes. Reduce pressure at room temperature.

Cut the ham into thin strips and chop the remaining onion. Brown the ham and onion together in the butter in a pan. Sprinkle with the flour and stir in the stock. Add seasoning and simmer for 5 minutes, then stir in the mustard.

Drain the lentils, keeping the liquid to make a soup. Put the lentils in a warm serving dish, pour the sauce over and sprinkle with parsley.
Serves 4

Stuffed Peppers

4 medium-sized green peppers
2 oz. (¼ cup) butter
1 large onion, finely chopped
¼ lb. (1 cup) mushrooms,
  chopped
2 medium-sized tomatoes,
  skinned and chopped

4 tablespoons (⅓ cup) fresh white
  breadcrumbs
2 oz. (½ cup) ground almonds
1 tablespoon chopped parsley
¼ teaspoon dried basil
salt and pepper

Remove the stalk of each pepper and cut out the core. Wash out any
remaining seeds. Melt the butter in a frying pan (skillet) and cook the onion
until soft, then add the mushrooms and tomatoes and cook a little longer.
Mix in the breadcrumbs, almonds, herbs and seasoning. Pack the stuffing
firmly into the peppers.

Put the trivet in the pressure cooker with ½ pint (1¼ cups) water. Either
stand the peppers on the trivet or in vegetable separators. Cover with
greased greaseproof (waxed) paper. Put on the lid and bring to HIGH (15
lb.) pressure and cook for 7 minutes. Reduce pressure at room
temperature.
Serves 4

Stuffed Marrow

1 medium-sized marrow (squash)
2 oz. (¼ cup) butter
1 onion, chopped
2 tomatoes, skinned and sliced

1 tablespoon rice
6 oz. (1 cup) cooked minced
  (ground) meat
salt and pepper

Peel the marrow, cut a slice from the stalk end and scoop out the centre
pulp. Melt 1 tablespoon of the butter in a frying pan (skillet) and
lightly fry the onion, tomatoes and rice for about 5 minutes. Add the
minced meat and seasoning and mix well. Fill the marrow with the mixture.

Put the trivet in the pressure cooker with ½ pint (1¼ cups) water. Place
the stuffed marrow on the trivet and replace the cut-off end. Put several
small knobs of butter along the length of the marrow. Cover with (waxed)
greaseproof paper. Put on the lid, bring to HIGH (15 lb.) pressure and
cook for 12 minutes. Reduce pressure in cold water.

Cut the marrow into thick slices and serve with a sauce, such as tomato
or cheese sauce.
Serves 4-6

CASSOULET, *page 60 (Photograph: Bisto)*

DESSERTS AND PUDDINGS

General instructions for cooking steamed puddings:

1. Any type of heatproof, watertight basin (mold) can be used. Metal and boilable plastics give the quickest results. If using china or ovenglass, add 5-10 minutes to the cooking time.

2. Grease the container well. It should be not more than two thirds full of pudding mixture, as the pudding needs space to rise.

3. Cover with greased foil or a double thickness of greased greaseproof (waxed) paper. Make a pleat in the foil or paper to allow the pudding to rise, tie it down securely, and make a handle of string.

4. Have the pressure cooker ready, containing the trivet, a little lemon juice or vinegar to prevent discoloration and at least 2 pints (5 cups) boiling water. Do not keep the water boiling while you prepare the pudding, as it will evaporate and there will not be enough to last the cooking time.

5. Lower the pudding on to the trivet.

6. For puddings containing a raising agent, a short steaming time is needed before pressure is built up to allow the raising agent to work and make the pudding light. To steam, put on the lid (without the weight) and lower the heat so that there is a steady but very gentle flow of steam from the centre vent. Steam on low heat for the time given in the recipe.

7. At the end of the steaming time, put on the weight and raise the heat to bring to LOW (5 lb.) pressure. Then lower the heat and cook in the normal way for the required time.

8. Reduce pressure at room temperature so that the pudding will remain light.

Note: If your cooker has only HIGH (15 lb.) pressure, you can obtain good results, particularly for suet puddings, at this pressure, but follow the pre-steaming instructions and reduce cooking time by about 10 minutes.

Lemon Pudding

Suet pastry:
8 oz. (2 cups) self-raising flour
½ teaspoon salt
4 oz. (½ cup) shredded suet
cold water to mix

1 lemon
8 oz. (1 cup) demerara sugar
1 oz. (2T) butter, cut into pieces

Mix the dry ingredients for the pastry and add enough water to make a pliable dough. Knead the dough lightly and roll out two thirds of it on a floured surface. Line a greased 2 pint (5 cup) pudding basin (mold) with this dough and roll out the remainder to form a lid.

Grate the lemon rind and remove the white pith. Chop the lemon flesh and mix it with the grated rind, the sugar and the butter. Place this filling in the lined basin (mold) and put on the pastry lid. Damp the edges and seal well.

Cover the basin (mold) and steam in the pressure cooker for 15 minutes (see page 66), then cook for 30 minutes at LOW (5 lb.) pressure. Reduce pressure at room temperature. Serve with custard or a sauce.

Serves 4-6

Apple and Cinnamon Layer Pudding

Suet pastry:
8 oz. (2 cups) self-raising flour
½ teaspoon salt
4 oz. (½ cup) shredded suet
cold water to mix

1 lb. apples
2 oz. (⅓ cup) sultanas (golden raisins)
1 teaspoon ground (powdered) cinnamon
castor (superfine) sugar

Mix the dry ingredients for the pastry and add enough water to make a pliable dough. Knead the dough lightly and roll it out on a floured surface. Divide it into four portions, each one a little larger than the last. Grease a 2 pint (5 cup) pudding basin (mold). Roll the smallest portion into a circle to fit the bottom of the pudding basin (mold). Roll out the other portions of dough into progressively larger circles.

Peel and slice the apples and mix with the sultanas, cinnamon and sugar to taste. Place the smallest circle of dough in the bottom of the basin (mold). Add a layer of fruit mixture, then another round of dough and continue like this, finishing with the largest round of dough.

Cover the basin (mold) and steam in the pressure cooker for 15 minutes (see page 66) then cook for 45 minutes at LOW (5 lb.) pressure. Reduce pressure at room temperature.

Dredge with castor (superfine) sugar before serving.

Serves 4-6

Peach Cap Pudding

glacé cherry
small can sliced peaches
6 oz. (1½ cups) self-raising flour
pinch of salt
6 oz. (¾ cup) butter

6 oz. (¾ cup) castor (superfine)
 sugar
3 eggs, beaten
angelica 'leaves' for decoration
 (optional)

Grease a 2½ pint (6¼ cup) basin (mold). Place the cherry in the centre of the base and arrange the drained peach slices round it. Sift the flour and salt into a bowl. Beat the butter with a wooden spoon until soft, add the sugar and beat again until light in colour and fluffy in texture. Beat in the eggs one at a time, together with a tablespoon of the flour. Stir in the remaining flour. Place the mixture over the fruit. Cover the basin (mold).

Steam the pudding in the pressure cooker for 20 minutes (see page 66) and cook for 50 minutes at LOW (5 lb.) pressure. Reduce pressure at room temperature. Turn out on to a hot plate, decorate the edge of the cherry with angelica 'leaves'. Serve with custard.
Serves 8

Crème Caramel

5 oz. (⅔ cup) sugar
¼ pint (⅔ cup) water
1 pint (2½ cups) milk

4 eggs, lightly whisked
vanilla essence to taste

Put 4 oz. (½ cup) of the sugar and the water in a small pan. Dissolve sugar slowly over gentle heat. Bring to the boil without stirring until it caramalizes or becomes golden brown in colour. Pour the mixture into four warmed heatproof bowls or cups, making sure that the bottom of each is covered. Allow to cool. Warm the milk.

Put the eggs, vanilla essence and remaining sugar in a bowl, pour on the warmed milk and stir. Pour the mixture over the cooled caramel. Tie on each bowl or cup a double thickness of greased greaseproof (waxed) paper. Put ½ pint (1¼ cups) water and the trivet in the pressure cooker. Stand the bowls or cups on the trivet. Put on the lid and bring to HIGH (15 lb.) pressure. Cook for 3 minutes. Reduce pressure at room temperature.

To serve hot, turn the crème caramel on to a hot dish. To serve cold, leave to set cold before turning out.
Serves 4

PEACH CAP PUDDING *(Photograph: McDougalls)*

Basic Egg Custard

¾ pint (2 cups) milk
2 large eggs
2 tablespoons (3T) castor
  (superfine) sugar

½ teaspoon vanilla essence
½ teaspoon ground (powdered)
  nutmeg

Warm the milk in a small pan. Whisk the eggs, sugar and vanilla essence in a bowl and pour on the warmed milk, stirring. Pour the mixture into a greased heatproof dish.

Put the trivet in the pressure cooker with ½ pint (1¼ cups) water and a few drops of lemon juice to prevent discoloration. Stand the dish on the trivet, sprinkle nutmeg on the custard and lay a double thickness of greaseproof (waxed) paper over the dish. Put on the lid and bring to HIGH (15 lb.) pressure. Cook for 5 minutes, then reduce pressure at room temperature. Serve hot or cold.
Serves 4

Bread Pudding

6 thick slices stale bread
1½ oz. (3T) butter, melted
2 oz. (¼ cup) brown sugar
½ teaspoon vanilla essence

3 oz. (½ cup) mixed dried fruit
1 teaspoon mixed spice
1 egg, beaten
milk to mix

Soak the bread in hot water for about 20 minutes. Squeeze out the water and beat until smooth. Stir in the melted butter, sugar and vanilla essence. Mix well. Add the dried fruit and mixed spice. Beat in the egg and, if necessary, sufficient milk to make a smooth consistency. Put the mixture into a greased 1½ pint (3¾ cup) loaf tin (pan) or basin (mold), leaving at least 1 inch space at top. Tie on a double thickness of greased greaseproof (waxed) paper.

Put the trivet and 1 pint (2½ cups) boiling water in the pressure cooker and steam for 5 minutes (see page 66). Then cook for 10 minutes at HIGH (15 lb.) pressure. Reduce pressure at room temperature.
Serves 4-6

Bread and Butter Pudding

3-4 thin slices of buttered bread
2 oz. (⅓ cup) dried fruit
ground (powdered) nutmeg or
  cinnamon
brown sugar for the top

Custard:
¾ pint (2 cups) milk
2 large eggs
2 tablespoons (3T) castor
  (superfine) sugar
½ teaspoon vanilla essence
ground (powdered) nutmeg

Cut the slices of bread into four and fill a greased flameproof dish with alternate layers of bread and dried fruit, sprinkling each layer with a little nutmeg or cinnamon. Make up the egg custard as in the basic recipe (see page 70), then pour it over the bread and butter. Cook as for egg custard.

Sprinkle the brown sugar over the cooked pudding and brown it lightly under a hot grill (broiler).
Serves 4

Pears in Red Wine

4 cooking pears
2 oz. (¼ cup) castor (superfine)
  sugar

½ pint (1¼ cups) red wine
2 teaspoons lemon juice
2 tablespoons (3T) redcurrant jelly

Peel, halve and core the pears. Arrange them in the pressure cooker and sprinkle over the sugar. Mix together the wine, lemon juice and redcurrant jelly and pour it over the fruit. Put on the lid and bring to HIGH (15 lb.) pressure. Cook for 4-8 minutes, depending on the size and hardness of the pears. Reduce pressure at room temperature.
Serves 4

Baked Stuffed Apples

4 medium-sized cooking apples
2 oz. (¼ cup) sugar
½ teaspoon ground (powdered)
  cinnamon

4 oz. (⅔ cup) sultanas (golden
  raisins)
4 cloves

Wash and core the apples. Mix together the sugar, cinnamon and sultanas. Fill the apples with this mixture and place a clove on top of each. Put the trivet and ½ pint (1¼ cups) water in the pressure cooker. Stand the apples on the trivet. Put on the lid, bring to HIGH (15 lb.) pressure and cook for 3-4 minutes. Reduce pressure at room temperature.
Serves 4

Lemon Pudding with Autumn Sauce

5 oz. (1¼ cups) self-raising flour
pinch of salt
3 oz. (¼ cup + 2T) butter
3 oz. (¼ cup + 2T) castor
 (superfine) sugar
grated rind of 1 lemon
1 oz. (¼ cup) chopped almonds
1 egg, beaten

milk to mix
Autumn Sauce:
1 lb. soft fruit (e.g. raspberries)
3-4 tablespoons (¼-⅓ cup) water
4 oz. (½ cup) castor (superfine)
 sugar
3 teaspoons arrowroot
¼ pint (⅔ cup) red wine

Sift the flour and salt into a bowl, then rub in the butter until the mixture resembles fine breadcrumbs. Stir in the sugar, lemon rind and almonds. Mix in the egg and just enough milk to make a smooth dropping consistency. Spoon the mixture into a greased 1½ pint (3¾ cup) pudding basin (mold) and tie on a double layer of greased greaseproof (waxed) paper.

Steam the pudding in the pressure cooker for 15 minutes (see page 66), then cook at LOW (5 lb.) pressure for 25 minutes. Reduce pressure at room temperature.

To make the sauce, cook the fruit with the water and sugar until soft, then press it through a sieve and return it to the pan. Mix the arrowroot with the wine and stir into the fruit. Bring to the boil, stirring, and simmer for 1 minute. Serve the pudding hot with the sauce poured over.
Serves 4-6

Chelsea Pudding

2 oz. (½ cup) self-raising flour
2 oz. (1 cup) fresh white
 breadcrumbs
2 oz. (¼ cup) shredded suet
2 oz. (⅓ cup) currants

2 oz. (⅓ cup) raisins
4 tablespoons (⅓ cup) treacle
 (molasses), warmed
4 tablespoons (⅓ cup) milk

Mix together the dry ingredients in a large bowl. Make a hollow in the centre and add the slightly warmed treacle, then gradually add the milk. Beat well. Pour the mixture into a greased 1 pint (2½ cup) pudding basin (mold). Tie on a double thickness of greased greaseproof (waxed) paper.

Steam the pudding in the pressure cooker for 15 minutes (see page 66), then cook at LOW (5 lb.) pressure for 30 minutes. Reduce pressure at room temperature. Serve hot with custard.
Serves 4

LEMON PUDDING WITH AUTUMN SAUCE *(Photograph: Home Baking Bureau)*

Steamed Banana Pudding with Lemon Sauce

4 oz. (½ cup) butter, softened
4 oz. (½ cup) castor (superfine) sugar
2 eggs, beaten
4 oz. (1 cup) self-raising flour
grated rind of 1 lemon

2 ripe bananas, sliced
Lemon sauce:
1 tablespoon custard powder
½ pint (1¼ cups) water
juice of 1 lemon
1 oz. (2T) sugar

Beat the butter and sugar together with a wooden spoon until light and creamy. Gradually beat in the eggs, adding a little flour after each addition. Using a metal spoon, fold in the lemon rind and remaining flour. Then stir in the bananas. Spoon the mixture into a greased 1½ pint (3¾ cup) pudding basin (mold). Tie on a double layer of greased greaseproof (waxed) paper.

Steam the pudding in the pressure cooker for 15 minutes (see page 66), then cook at LOW (5 lb.) pressure for 35 minutes. Reduce pressure at room temperature.

To make the sauce, blend the custard powder with a little water until smooth, then stir in the remaining water. Bring it to the boil in a small pan, stirring, and cook until the sauce thickens. Add the lemon juice and sugar.

Serves 4-6

Spicy Pudding

4 oz. (1 cup) self-raising flour
pinch of salt
3 oz. (¼ cup + 2T) margarine
3 oz. (¼ cup + 2T) sugar
4 oz. (2 cups) fresh brown breadcrumbs
4 oz. (⅔ cup) sultanas (golden raisins)

2 teaspoons ground (powdered) cinnamon
1 teaspoon ground (powdered) nutmeg
1 egg, beaten
milk to mix

Sift the flour and salt into a bowl and rub in the margarine until the mixture resembles fine breadcrumbs. Add the remaining dry ingredients and mix together with the egg and sufficient milk to form a smooth dropping consistency. Put the mixture in a greased 1½ pint (3¾ cup) pudding basin (mold) and tie on a double layer of greased greaseproof (waxed) paper.

Steam the pudding in the pressure cooker for 15 minutes (see page 66), then cook at LOW (5 lb.) pressure for 35 minutes. Reduce pressure at room temperature. Serve with custard.

Serves 4

Fresh Fruit Pudding

6 oz. (1½ cups) self-raising flour
pinch of salt
3 oz. (⅔ cup) shredded suet

water to mix
1 lb. fruit for filling (see below)
sugar to taste

Mix together the flour, salt and suet and add enough water to give a firm dough. Roll out two thirds of the pastry and use it to line a greased 1½ pint (3¾ cup) pudding basin (mold). Put the fruit inside with sugar to taste. Roll out the remaining dough to form a lid, damp the edges and seal well. Tie on a double thickness of greased greaseproof (waxed) paper.

Steam the pudding in the pressure cooker for 15 minutes (see page 66), then cook at LOW (5 lb.) pressure for 35 minutes. Reduce pressure at room temperature.

Fruit filling:

If using soft fruits, do not add any water, just add sugar, golden syrup or honey to sweeten. Wash hard fruits and leave them rather wet, then add 2 or 3 tablespoons (3T or ¼ cup) water or syrup.

Spring: rhubarb, or rhubarb and orange, or rhubarb and dried figs. Cut the rhubarb into pieces. If using orange, add the finely grated peel and chopped sections of the fruit (allow 1 orange to 1 lb. rhubarb). Allow about 4 oz. (¼ cup) chopped figs to 1 lb. rhubarb.

Summer: blackcurrants, gooseberries, cherries, or a mixture of all summer fruits.

Autumn: blackberry and apple, damsons, plums, greengages, quinces and apples.

Winter: apples.

Serves 4

Jam Cap Pudding

3 oz. (¼ cup + 2T) butter,
  softened
3 oz. (¼ cup + 2T) castor
  (superfine) sugar
5 oz. (1¼ cups) self-raising flour

pinch of salt
2 eggs, beaten
1 tablespoon milk
2-3 (3-4T) tablespoons jam

Beat the butter with a wooden spoon, then add the sugar and continue beating until the mixture is light and fluffy. Sift the flour with the salt into a bowl. Add the eggs gradually to the creamed mixture with a little of the flour. Stir, then beat thoroughly. Stir in the milk and a little flour, then beat again. Fold in the rest of the flour.

Grease a 1½ pint (3¾ cup) pudding basin (mold) and put the jam in the bottom. Spoon the pudding mixture over the jam. Tie on a double layer of greased greaseproof (waxed) paper.

Steam the pudding in the pressure cooker for 15 minutes (see page 66), then cook at LOW (5 lb.) pressure for 25 minutes. Reduce pressure at room temperature. Serve with jam sauce as described on page 80.

Serves 4-6

Marshmallow Pears

4 dessert pears, not too ripe
¼ pint (⅔ cup) water
4 tablespoons (⅓ cup) sugar
little lemon juice

pinch of ground (powdered)
  ginger or cinnamon
4 pink and 4 white marshmallows

Peel, halve and core the pears. Gently heat the water, sugar and lemon juice in the open pressure cooker until the sugar melts, then boil until the syrup thickens. Put in the pears, cut side up, put on the lid and bring to HIGH (15 lb.) pressure. Cook for 2-3 minutes, according to ripeness. Reduce pressure in cold water.

Lift out the pears with a draining spoon and allow the syrup to drain off. Put them in a shallow flameproof dish, place a marshmallow on each and heat gently under the grill (broiler) until the marshmallows begin to melt.

Serves 4

JAM CAP PUDDING *(Photograph: McDougalls)*

Tangy Chocolate Pudding with Chocolate Sauce

6 oz. (1½ cups) self-raising flour
4 oz. (½ cup) margarine
4 oz. (½ cup) soft brown sugar
1 oz. (¼ cup) cocoa powder
1 tablespoon hot water
2 eggs, beaten
grated rind of 1 orange
1-2 tablespoons milk

1 orange, sliced for decoration
Chocolate sauce:
4 oz. (½ cup) soft brown sugar
2 oz. (½ cup) cocoa powder
¼ pint (⅔ cup) water
juice of 1 orange
1 oz. (2T) butter

Sift the flour into a bowl. Using a wooden spoon, beat the margarine and sugar together in a large mixing bowl until light and creamy. Mix the cocoa powder with hot water and beat into the mixture. Gradually add the eggs with a little of the flour, beating well between each addition. Then fold in the remaining flour and orange rind. Stir in just enough milk to give a dropping consistency. Put the mixture in a greased 1½ pint (3¾ cup) pudding basin (mold) and tie on a double thickness of greased greaseproof (waxed) paper.

Steam the pudding in the pressure cooker for 15 minutes (see page 66), then cook at LOW (5 lb.) pressure for 25 minutes. Reduce the pressure at room temperature.

To make the sauce; place all the ingredients in a pan and heat slowly, stirring, until the sugar has dissolved. Then boil rapidly for 2-3 minutes until the sauce coats the back of a wooden spoon.

Turn the pudding out on to a serving dish and arrange halved orange slices round it. Pour a little of the sauce over the top and serve the rest separately.
Serves 4-6

Festive Orange Pudding with Sherry Sauce

2 large oranges
3 oz. (1½ cups) stoned dates
1 cooking apple, peeled and cored
1 large carrot, scraped
2½ oz. (1¼ cups) fresh white
  breadcrumbs
3 oz. (¾ cup) plain (all-purpose)
  flour
2 oz. (¼ cup) soft brown sugar
3 oz. (¼ cup + 2T) shredded suet

3 oz. (½ cup) seedless raisins
½ teaspoon mixed spice
pinch of salt
1 egg, beaten
Sherry sauce:
grated rind and juice of 2 oranges
2 oz. (¼ cup) sugar
1 tablespoon arrowroot
4 tablespoons (⅓ cup) medium
  sherry

To make the pudding, pare the rind from one orange, cut it into thin strips and reserve for decoration. Finely grate the rind from the other orange. Remove the pith and pips from the orange and finely mince (grind) the orange flesh with the dates, apple and carrot. Alternatively, finely chop the orange flesh and dates, and grate the apple and carrot.

Mix together in a large bowl the breadcrumbs, flour, sugar, suet, raisins, spice, salt and grated orange rind. Stir in the fruit mixture. Add the egg to the mixture, and stir well until the ingredients are thoroughly mixed. Put the mixture in a greased 1½ pint (3¾ cup) pudding basin (mold) and tie on a double layer of greased greaseproof (waxed) paper.

Have the pressure cooker ready with the trivet and 3 pints (7½ cups) boiling water and a little lemon juice in it, but do not keep the water boiling while you prepare the pudding or there will not be enough to last the cooking time. Stand the pudding on the trivet, put on the lid of the cooker and lower the heat so that a very gentle but steady flow of steam escapes from the centre vent. Let it steam like this (without the weight) on low heat for 20 minutes. Then put on the weight and raise the heat to bring to HIGH (15 lb.) pressure. When pressure is reached, lower the heat and cook in the usual way for 1¾ hours. Reduce pressure at room temperature.

To make the sauce, make up the orange juice to ½ pint (1¼ cups) with water and put it in a pan with the grated rind and the sugar. Heat gently until the sugar is dissolved. Blend the arrowroot with 2 tablespoons (3T) water and add it to the pan. Bring to the boil, stirring, and cook until the sauce thickens and clears. Stir in the sherry.

Turn the pudding out on to a serving dish, pour some of the sauce over the top and decorate with the strips of orange peel. Serve the remaining sauce separately.

Serves 4-6

Note: Storage time for this pudding is limited, but it will keep for two weeks in a refrigerator. To reheat, put it on the trivet in the pressure cooker containing 1 pint (2½ cups) boiling water and a little lemon juice and cook at HIGH (15 lb.) pressure for 20 minutes.

Delicious Pudding

4 oz. (1 cup) self-raising flour
2 oz. (¼ cup) margarine
2 oz. (¼ cup) sugar
1 oz. (3T) currants
1 oz. (3T) raisins
1 egg, beaten with 1 tablespoon
  milk

2 tablespoons (3T) jam
Apricot or raspberry sauce:
6 oz. (½ cup) jam (apricot or
  raspberry)
2 tablespoons (3T) water
½ teaspoon lemon juice

Sift the flour into a bowl, then rub in the margarine and add the sugar and fruit. Mix in the beaten egg and milk.

Grease a 1 pint (2½ cup) pudding basin (mold) and put the jam in the bottom. Spoon the mixture into the basin (mold) and tie on a double thickness of greased greaseproof (waxed) paper.

Steam the pudding in the pressure cooker for 15 minutes (see page 66), then cook for 25 minutes. Reduce pressure at room temperature.

To make the sauce, blend the jam with the water and lemon juice. Heat then sieve to give a smooth sauce. Serve with the pudding.
Serves 4-6

Rice Pudding

½ oz. (1T) butter
1 pint (2½ cups) milk
2 oz. (⅓ cup) pudding rice

2 oz. (¼ cup) sugar
½ teaspoon ground (powdered)
  nutmeg

Melt the butter in the open pressure cooker. Pour in the milk and quickly bring to the boil. Add the rice and sugar and boil again. Lower the heat until the milk is simmering. Put on the lid and bring to HIGH (15 lb.) pressure on low heat. Cook for 12 minutes.

Reduce pressure at room temperature. Stir the pudding, put it in a flameproof dish, sprinkle with nutmeg and brown under a hot grill (broiler) or in the oven for a few minutes.
Serves 3-4

DELICIOUS PUDDING (Photograph: Be-Ro)

Summer Fruit Pudding

4 oz. (1 cup) self-raising flour
pinch of salt
6 oz. (¾ cup) melted butter
4 oz. (2 cups) fresh white
  breadcrumbs
1 large egg, beaten
milk

1 lb. stewed fruit (e.g. plums,
  cherries, redcurrants,
  blackcurrants)
sugar to taste
1 teaspoon lemon juice
2 teaspoons arrowroot or
  cornflour (cornstarch)

Sift the flour and salt into a bowl and stir in the melted butter. Add the
breadcrumbs and mix to a stiff dough with the egg and a little milk. Roll out
two thirds of the dough into a circle and use it to line a greased 1½ pint (3¾
cup) pudding basin (mold). Strain the fruit and put it in the lined basin
(mold). Add sugar to taste and the lemon juice. Roll out the remaining
dough to form a lid. Damp the edges of dough and seal well. Tie on a
double thickness of greased greaseproof (waxed) paper.

    Steam the pudding in the pressure cooker for 15 minutes (see page 66),
then cook at LOW (5 lb.) pressure for 40 minutes. Reduce pressure at
room temperature. Use the juice from the strained fruit to make a sauce:
add the arrowroot or cornflour blended with cold water and bring it to the
boil, stirring, to thicken. Serve the sauce with the pudding.
Serves 4

Apricot Snow

6 oz. (1 cup) dried apricots
little lemon juice
sugar to taste

3 egg whites
blanched, shredded almonds to
  decorate

Wash the apricots in hot water and drain. Then put them in a bowl, pour over ½ pint (1¼ cups) boiling water and leave them to soak, covered, for 10 minutes. Put the apricots in the pressure cooker with the soaking liquid, lemon juice and sugar to taste. Put on the lid and bring to HIGH (15 lb.) pressure, then cook for 3 minutes. Reduce pressure at room temperature.

Drain the apricots, reserving the juice, and sieve the fruit. Add a scant tablespoon of the juice to the purée, taste and add more sugar if necessary. Beat the egg whites until stiff, then gently fold them into the apricot purée. Put the mixture in a greased ovenproof serving dish and bake for 15-20 minutes in the centre of the oven at 375°F, Gas Mark 5, until golden brown. At the same time brown the almonds on a baking sheet in the bottom of the oven. Sprinkle the browned almonds over the pudding before serving. Boil up the reserved apricot juice until it is thick, add a little lemon juice and serve separately.

Serves 4

Christmas Pudding

6 oz. (1 cup) currants
6 oz. (1 cup) sultanas (golden
  raisins)
12 oz. (2 cups) seedless raisins
4 oz. (⅔ cup) mixed (candied)
  peel
1 oz. (¼ cup) ground almonds
2 oz. (½ cup) chopped almonds
4 oz. (1 cup) plain (all-purpose)
  flour
8 oz. (4 cups) fresh white
  breadcrumbs

8 oz. (1 cup) shredded suet
8 oz. (1 cup) soft brown sugar
½ teaspoon mixed spice
¼ teaspoon ground (powdered)
  nutmeg
juice and finely grated rind of
  1 lemon
4 eggs, beaten
¼ pint (⅔ cup) brown ale or stout

Mix together the fruit and dry ingredients. Add the lemon juice, eggs and brown ale and stir well until all the ingredients are thoroughly mixed. Divide the mixture between 5 greased 1 pint (2½ cup) pudding basins (molds) and press down well. Place a circle of greased greaseproof (waxed) paper on each pudding, then cover with foil and secure with string.

Put 2¼ pints (5¾ cups) water in the pressure cooker, and bring it to the boil. Place one pudding on the base of the pressure cooker, then place the trivet on top, and stand another pudding on the trivet. Put the lid on the pressure cooker and bring back to the boil. Then lower the heat so that a steady but very gentle flow of steam escapes through the vent. Keep the heat low and steam like this, without weight, for 15 minutes. Then increase the heat, put on the weight and bring to HIGH (15 lb.) pressure. Cook for a further 1¾ hours.

Reduce pressure at room temperature. Remove the foil covers from the puddings, and re-cover firmly with new foil. The puddings should be stored in a cool dry place. When required, reheat the puddings in the pressure cooker for 20 minutes at HIGH (15 lb.) pressure.
Makes five 1 lb. puddings

CHRISTMAS PUDDING *(Photograph: Atora)*

JAMS AND MARMALADES

Testing for a set

1. The most accurate method is the temperature test. When the sugar temperature reaches 221°F, the jam (or marmalade) should be set.
2. Stir the jam (or marmalade) with a wooden spoon. Turn the spoon in the hand to cool it slightly, then allow the jam (or marmalade) to drop; setting point is reached when it partly sets on the spoon.
3. Put a little of the jam (or marmalade) on a cold saucer and allow it to cool. Push a finger across the top of the jam (or marmalade); if it wrinkles, a set has been obtained. Remember to take the cooker off the heat when using this method, or the jam may boil too long.

Seville Orange Marmalade

1 ½ lb. Seville oranges　　　　　*1 pint (2 ½ cups) water*
juice of 1 large lemon　　　　　*3 lb. sugar, warmed*

Wash the fruit, then cut it in half and squeeze out the juice. Tie the pith and pips in a muslin bag and shred the peel. Soak the peel and the muslin bag in the water overnight.

Put the peel, muslin bag and the water in the pressure cooker. Put on the lid and bring to HIGH (15 lb.) pressure. Cook for 10-15 minutes, according to the thickness of the peel. Reduce pressure at room temperature.

The peel must be really tender before the sugar is added. To test, let it cool, then press a piece of peel between thumb and forefinger.

When it is cool enough to handle, take out the muslin bag and squeeze the juice from it into the cooker. Then add the warmed sugar. Stir over gentle heat until the sugar is dissolved, then boil it rapidly in the open cooker until setting point is reached (see above). Skim if necessary and let the marmalade cool until skin starts to form before pouring it into warm, dry jars. This prevents the peel rising in the jar. Cover each jar immediately with a waxed disc; when it is cool, cover with cellophane or a lid.

Makes about 5 lb. marmalade

Grapefruit Marmalade

1½ lb. grapefruit
3-4 lemons

1 pint (2½ cups) water
4 lb. (8 cups) sugar, warmed

Make as for Seville orange marmalade (see page 86), but cut up the lemons and use all the fruit, not just the juice. Cook for 10 minutes at HIGH (15 lb.) pressure.
Makes 6½-7 lb. marmalade

Lemon Marmalade

1½ lb. lemons
1 pint (2½ cups) water

3 lb. (6 cups) sugar, warmed

Make as for Seville orange marmalade (see page 86), cooking for 8 minutes at HIGH (15 lb.) pressure.
Makes about 5 lb. marmalade

Blackcurrant Jam

2 lb. blackcurrants
1 pint (2½ cups) water

3 lb. (6 cups) sugar, warmed

Wash the fruit and remove the stalks. Put the fruit in the pressure cooker with the water. Do not have it more than half full. Put on the lid and bring to MEDIUM (10 lb.) pressure. Cook for 3-4 minutes, according to ripeness of the fruit. Reduce pressure at room temperature.

Add the warmed sugar and dissolve over gentle heat in the open cooker. Then boil the fruit and sugar rapidly in the open cooker until setting point is reached (see page 86). Skim if necessary. Leave the jam until a skin forms (this will prevent the fruit rising to the top of the jars), then pour it into dry warm jars. Cover immediately with waxed discs. When the jam is cool, cover with cellophane or lids.
Makes about 5 lb. jam

Apple and Ginger Jam

3 lb. apples, washed and
  quartered
rind and juice of 1 large lemon

¾ pint (2 cups) water
ground (powdered) ginger
sugar (see recipe)

Put the apples in the pressure cooker with the lemon rind, juice and water.
Put on the lid and bring to MEDIUM (10 lb.) pressure. Cook for 5 minutes.
Reduce pressure at room temperature.

Sieve the apple, measure the purée and add 1 teaspoon ginger and 1 lb.
(2 cups) sugar to every pint (2½ cups) of apple purée. Return the purée to
the cooker with the ginger and sugar and continue as for Blackcurrant jam
(see page 87).
Makes about 4 lb. jam

Fresh Apricot Jam

2 lb. fresh apricots
½ pint (1 ¼ cups) water

juice of ½ lemon
2 lb. (4 cups) sugar, warmed

Wash the apricots and remove the stones. Crack a few stones to remove
the kernels and blanch them by dipping them into hot water. Put the fruit,
water, lemon juice and kernels in the pressure cooker and put on the lid.
Bring to MEDIUM (10 lb.) pressure and cook for 4 minutes. Reduce
pressure at room temperature and continue as for Blackcurrant jam (see
page 87).
Makes 3-3½ lb. jam

Dried Apricot Jam

1 lb. dried apricots
2 pints (5 cups) boiling water
juice of 1 lemon

3 lb. (6 cups) sugar, warmed
2 oz. (½ cup) blanched almonds

Wash the apricots, cut them up and put them in the pressure cooker. Pour
the boiling water into the cooker, cover and leave for 1 hour to soak. Add
the lemon juice, put on the lid and bring to HIGH (15 lb.) pressure. Cook
for 10 minutes. Reduce pressure at room temperature, then continue as
for Blackcurrant jam (see page 87), adding the almonds with the sugar.
Makes 4-5 lb. jam

Plum Jam

3 lb. fresh red plums
½ pint (1 ¼ cups) water

3 lb. (6 cups) sugar, warmed

Wash the plums, cut in half and remove the stones. Crack about 10 of these stones and remove the kernels. Blanch the kernels in boiling water for 5 minutes then split each one in half.

Place the fruit, water and kernels in the pressure cooker. Put on the lid, bring to MEDIUM (10 lb.) pressure and cook for 4 minutes. Reduce pressure at room temperature.

Add the warmed sugar and dissolve over gentle heat in the open cooker. Then boil the fruit and syrup rapidly until setting point is reached (see page 86).

Leave the jam to cool until the fruit is suspended in the syrup before turning into dry warmed jars. This prevents the fruit from rising to the top of the jars. Cover immediately with waxed discs. Leave to cool completely before covering the jars with cellophane.

Makes about 5 lb. jam

Blackberry and Apple Jam

1 lemon
1 lb. tart cooking apples, washed
2 lb. blackberries, washed and
 hulled

¼ pint (⅔ cup) water
3 lb. (6 cups) sugar, warmed

Using a potato peeler, remove the rind from the lemon and reserve. Cut the lemon in half and squeeze the juice.

Peel, quarter and core the apples. Tie the apple peel, core and lemon rind in a small muslin (cheesecloth) bag.

Place the apples, blackberries and water in the pressure cooker. Add the muslin bag. Put on the lid and bring to MEDIUM (10 lb.) pressure. Cook for 4-5 minutes depending on ripeness of the fruit then reduce pressure at room temperature. Remove the muslin bag.

Add the lemon juice with the sugar and dissolve over low heat in the open pressure cooker. Then boil the fruit and syrup rapidly in the open cooker until setting point is reached (see page 86). Skim if necessary.

Leave the jam to cool slightly before pouring into dry warm jars. Cover with waxed discs. When the jam is cool, cover with cellophane or lids.

Makes about 5 lb. jam

INDEX

INDEX

The editor would like to thank The Prestige Group for their assistance in testing recipes for this book.